THE USBORNE ILLUSTRATED
DICTIONARY OF
PHYSICS

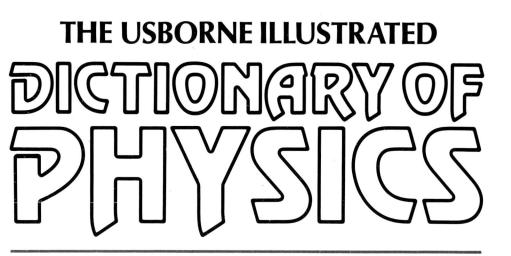

**Chris Oxlade, Corinne Stockley
and Jane Wertheim**

**Designed by Chris Scollen,
Stephen Wright and Roger Berry**

Additional designs by Iain Ashman, Anne Sharples
and Camilla Luff

Scientific advisors:
Dr. Tom Petersen,
John Hawkins
and Dr. John Durell.

Illustrated by:
Kuo Kang Chen, Guy Smith
and Caroline Ewen.

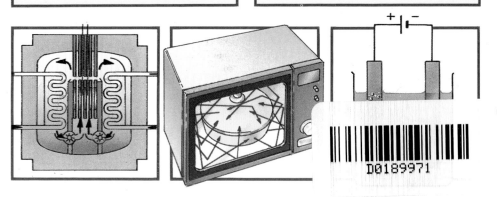

D0189971

Contents

First published in 1986 Usborne Publishing Ltd, Usborne House 83-85 Saffron Hill, London EC1N 8RT, England

© Copyright 1986 Usborne Publishing Ltd

The name Usborne and the device are Trade Marks of Usborne Publishing Ltd.

Printed in Great Britain

About this book

Physics is the science dealing with the properties of matter, the different forms of energy and how they affect the world around us. This book divides the subject up, using six main colour-coded sections.

Blue section / Mechanics and general physics – forces, energy and properties of substances.

Yellow section / Heat energy, its effect and how it is measured and transferred.

Red section / Wave energy, properties of waves and specific kinds of wave.

Green section / Static and current electricity, magnets and magnetism.

Pink section / Atomic and nuclear structure, properties and energy. Radioactivity, fission and fusion.

Black and white section / Charts and tables relating to topics earlier in the book. Also information on treatment of experimental results.

How to use this book

This book can be used as a dictionary, or as a revision handbook. The definitions are arranged thematically, that is, all the words to do with the same subject are grouped together, in most cases on two facing pages. These subjects are listed as contents on page 2. The index on pages 116-128 forms the dictionary reference section. It is an alphabetical list of all the individual definitions in the book, giving page numbers for both main entries and supplementary entries. See page 116 for more about the use of the index.

Key to use of the book

1. Every main definition is preceded by a dot, and the entry word is printed in bold type, e.g.:

   • **Elasticity**.

2. Any singulars or plurals (which are not simply the addition of a letter s) follow straight after an entry, e.g.:

   • **Nucleus** (pl. **nuclei**).

3. Any synonyms of the word also follow immediately, e.g.:

   • **Screening** or **shielding**.
   (only one synonym)

   • **Relative atomic mass**. Also called **atomic mass** or **atomic weight**.
   (more than one synonym)

4. Many other words are also printed in bold. These are either defined where they appear, or the bold type is a sign that their own definitions can be found elsewhere on the same two pages.

5. If a word is in bold type and has an asterisk (*), it is defined elsewhere in the book and is in the footnote at the bottom of the page.

6. This is a typical footnote:

   * **Dip circle**, 73 (**Inclination**); **Nucleus**, 82; **Dipole**, **Induced magnetism**, 71.

   a) The definition of **dip circle** can be found inside the text of the main definition entry **Inclination** on page 73.

   b) The entry word **nucleus** can be found on page 82, so this is the word given in the footnote, even though the plural **nuclei*** may have been what appeared in the text.

Atoms and molecules

The Greeks believed that all matter was made up of tiny particles which they called **atoms**. This idea has since been expanded and theories such as the **kinetic theory** have been developed which can be used to explain the physical nature and behaviour of substances in much greater detail. Matter can exist in three different **physical states**. The state of a substance depends on the nature of the substance, its temperature and the pressure exerted on it. Changes between states are caused by changes in the pressure or temperature (for more about this, see **changes of state**, page 30).

- **Atom**. The smallest part of a substance which can exist and still retain the properties of the substance. The internal structure of the atom is explained on pages 82-83. Atoms are extremely small, having radii of about 10^{-10}m and masses of about 10^{-25}kg. They can form **ions*** (electrically charged particles) by the loss or gain of **electrons*** (see **ionization**, page 88).

- **Molecule**. The smallest naturally-occurring particle of a substance. Molecules can consist of any number of **atoms**, from one (e.g. neon) to many thousands (e.g. proteins), all held together by **electromagnetic forces***. All the molecules of a pure sample of a substance contain the same atoms in the same arrangement.

- **Element**. A substance which cannot be split into simpler substances by a chemical reaction. All **atoms** of the same element have the same number of **protons*** in their **nuclei*** (see **atomic number**, page 82).

- **Compound**. A substance whose **molecules** contain the **atoms** of two or more **elements**, chemically bonded together, and which can thus be split into simpler substances. A **mixture** has no chemical bonding and is therefore not a compound.

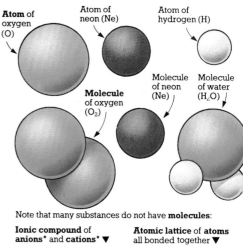

Atom of oxygen (O)

Atom of neon (Ne)

Atom of hydrogen (H)

Molecule of oxygen (O_2)

Molecule of neon (Ne)

Molecule of water (H_2O)

Note that many substances do not have **molecules**:

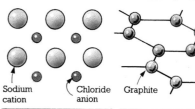

Ionic compound of **anions*** and **cations*** ▼

Atomic lattice of **atoms** all bonded together ▼

Sodium cation

Chloride anion

Graphite

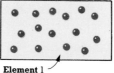

Element 1

Element 2

Mixture of 1 and 2 – no chemical bonding

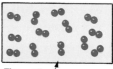

Compound of 1 and 2 – elements bonded together

* Anions, Cations, 88 (Ionization); Electromagnetic force, 6; Electrons, 83; Ions, 88 (Ionization); Nucleus, Protons, 82.

- **Solid state**. A **state** in which a substance has a definite volume and shape and resists forces which try to change these.

- **Liquid state**. A **state** in which a substance flows and takes up the shape of its containing vessel. It is between the **solid** and **gaseous** states.

- **Gaseous state**. A **state** in which a substance expands to fill its containing vessel. Substances in this state have a relatively low density.

- **Gas**. A substance in the **gaseous state** which is above its **critical temperature** and so cannot be turned into a liquid just by increasing the pressure – the temperature must be lowered first, to create a **vapour**.

- **Vapour**. A substance in the **gaseous state** which is below its **critical temperature** (see **gas**) and so can be turned into a liquid by an increase in pressure alone.

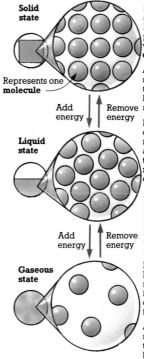

Solid state
Molecules vibrate about mean positions, having **molecular potential energy*** and **vibrational kinetic energy***

Represents one molecule

Average energy of molecule much less than that needed by it to break free from other molecules.

Add energy | Remove energy

Energy added breaks down regular pattern – molecules can move around and thus have **translational** and **rotational kinetic energy*** as well.

Liquid state

Average energy of molecule just about that needed for it to break free from neighbouring molecules, only to be captured by the next ones along.

Add energy | Remove energy

Molecules have very large separation – they move virtually independently of each other – **intermolecular forces*** can be ignored.

Gaseous state

Average energy of molecule much greater than a molecule needs to break free from others.

The kinetic theory

The **kinetic theory** explains the behaviour of the different physical states in terms of the motion of **molecules**. In brief, it states that the molecules of solids are closest together, have least energy and so move the least, those of liquids are further apart with more energy, and those of gases are furthest apart with most energy. See above right.

- **Brownian motion**. The observed random motion of small particles in

Brownian motion of smoke particles as they are hit by **molecules** in the air.

water or air. It supports the kinetic theory, as it could be said to be due to impact with unseen water or air **molecules**.

- **Diffusion**. The mixing of two gases, vapours or liquids over a period of time. It supports the kinetic theory, since the particles must be moving to mix, and gases can be seen to diffuse faster than liquids.

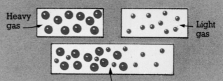

Heavy gas

Light gas

Light gas diffuses faster than heavy one

- **Graham's law of diffusion**. States that, at constant temperature and pressure, the rate of **diffusion** of a **gas** is inversely proportional to the square root of its density.

$$\text{Rate of diffusion} \propto \sqrt{\frac{1}{\text{density of gas}}}$$

Forces

A **force** influences the shape and motion of an object. A single force will change its velocity (i.e. **accelerate*** it). Two equal and opposite forces will change its shape or size. It is a **vector quantity***, having both magnitude and direction, and is measured in **newtons**. The main types of force are **gravitational**, **magnetic**, **electric** and **nuclear**. See pages 104-107 for a comparison of the first three of these.

Forces are shown by arrowed lines (the length represents magnitude and the arrow direction).

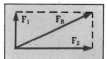

Effect of F_1 and F_2 is the same as F_R (the **resultant force**). F_1 and F_2 are the **components** of F_R.

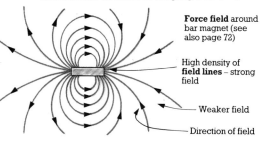

Force W resolved into two **components**

Component parallel to slope

Component at right angles to slope

- **Newton (N)**. The **SI unit*** of force. One newton is the force needed to accelerate a mass of 1 kg by 1 m s^{-2}.

Force field around bar magnet (see also page 72)

High density of **field lines** – strong field

Weaker field

Direction of field

- **Force field**. The region in which a force has an effect. The maximum distance over which a force has an effect is the **range** of the force. Force fields are represented by lines with arrows to show their strength and direction (see also pages 58 and 72).

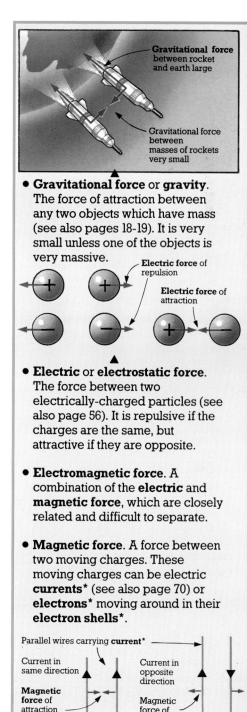

Gravitational force between rocket and earth large

Gravitational force between masses of rockets very small

- **Gravitational force** or **gravity**. The force of attraction between any two objects which have mass (see also pages 18-19). It is very small unless one of the objects is very massive.

Electric force of repulsion

Electric force of attraction

- **Electric** or **electrostatic force**. The force between two electrically-charged particles (see also page 56). It is repulsive if the charges are the same, but attractive if they are opposite.

- **Electromagnetic force**. A combination of the **electric** and **magnetic force**, which are closely related and difficult to separate.

- **Magnetic force**. A force between two moving charges. These moving charges can be electric **currents*** (see also page 70) or **electrons*** moving around in their **electron shells***.

Parallel wires carrying **current***

Current in same direction

Magnetic force of attraction

Current in opposite direction

Magnetic force of repulsion

- **Intermolecular forces**. The **electromagnetic forces** between two molecules. The strength and direction of the forces vary with the separation of the molecules (see picture, right).

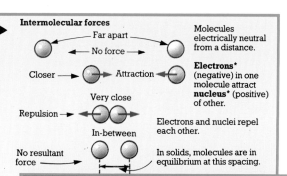

Intermolecular forces

Far apart — No force

Closer → Attraction

Very close

Repulsion →

In-between

No resultant force

Molecules electrically neutral from a distance.

Electrons* (negative) in one molecule attract **nucleus*** (positive) of other.

Electrons and nuclei repel each other.

In solids, molecules are in equilibrium at this spacing.

- **Tension**. Equal and opposite forces which, when applied to the ends of an object, increase its length. They are resisted by the **intermolecular force** of attraction.

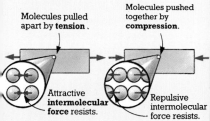

Molecules pulled apart by **tension**.

Molecules pushed together by **compression**.

Attractive **intermolecular force** resists.

Repulsive intermolecular force resists.

- **Compression**. Equal and opposite forces which decrease the length of an object. They are opposed by the **intermolecular force** of repulsion.

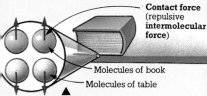

Contact force (repulsive **intermolecular force**)

Molecules of book
Molecules of table

- **Contact force**. The **intermolecular force** of repulsion between the molecules of two objects when they touch.

- **Nuclear force**. The force of attraction between all the particles of an atomic nucleus (the **protons*** and **neutrons***). It prevents the **electric force** of repulsion between the protons from pushing the nucleus apart (see also page 84).

- **Frictional force** or **friction**. The force which acts to oppose the motion of two touching surfaces over each other, caused by the **intermolecular force** of attraction between the molecules of the surfaces. There are two types, the **limiting** and the **dynamic frictional force**.

- **Limiting** or **static frictional force**. The maximum value of the **frictional force** between two surfaces. It occurs when the two surfaces are on the point of sliding over each other.

- **Dynamic frictional force** or **sliding frictional force**. The value of the **frictional force** when one surface is sliding over another at constant speed. It is slightly less than the **limiting frictional force**.

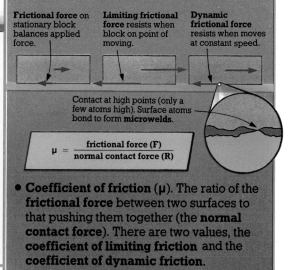

Frictional force on stationary block balances applied force.

Limiting frictional force resists when block on point of moving.

Dynamic frictional force resists when moves at constant speed.

Contact at high points (only a few atoms high). Surface atoms bond to form **microwelds**.

$$\mu = \frac{\text{frictional force (F)}}{\text{normal contact force (R)}}$$

- **Coefficient of friction (μ)**. The ratio of the **frictional force** between two surfaces to that pushing them together (the **normal contact force**). There are two values, the **coefficient of limiting friction** and the **coefficient of dynamic friction**.

Energy

Work is done when a force moves an object. **Energy** is the capacity to do work. When work is done on or by an object, it gains or loses energy respectively. Energy exists in many different forms and can change between them (energy **conversion** or **transformation**), but cannot be created or destroyed (**law of conservation of energy**). The **SI unit*** of energy and work is the **joule (J)**.

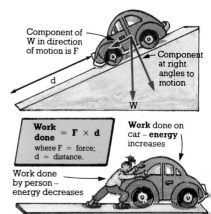

Component of W in direction of motion is F

Component at right angles to motion

d

W

| **Work done** $= \mathbf{F} \times \mathbf{d}$ |
| where F = force; d = distance. |

Work done on car – **energy** increases

Work done by person – energy decreases

- **Potential energy (P.E.)**. The energy of an object due to its position in a **force field***, which it has because work has been done to put it in that position. The energy has been "stored up". The three forms of potential energy are **gravitational potential energy**, **electromagnetic potential energy** and **nuclear potential energy** (depending on the force involved).

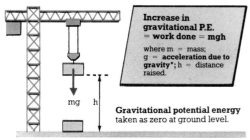

Increase in gravitational P.E. = work done = mgh

where m = mass; g = **acceleration due to gravity***; h = distance raised.

mg   h

Gravitational potential energy taken as zero at ground level.

- **Gravitational potential energy**. The **potential energy** associated with the position of an object relative to a mass which exerts a **gravitational force*** on it. If the object is moved further from the mass (e.g. an object being lifted on the earth), work is done on the body and its gravitational potential energy is raised.

- **Electromagnetic potential energy**. The **potential energy** associated with ▶ the position of a body in a **force field*** created by an **electromagnetic force***.

- **Elastic potential energy** or **strain energy**. An example of the **molecular potential energy**, stored as a result of stretching or compressing an object. It is the work done against the **intermolecular force***.

- **Molecular potential energy**. The **electromagnetic potential energy** associated with the position of molecules relative to one another. It is increased when work is done against the **intermolecular force***.

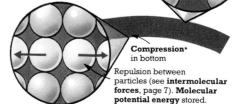

▶ **Elastic potential energy** stored when rod bent.

Tension* in top

Attraction between particles (see **intermolecular forces**, page 7). **Molecular potential energy** stored.

Compression* in bottom

Repulsion between particles (see **intermolecular forces**, page 7). **Molecular potential energy** stored.

- **Chemical energy**. Energy stored in substances such as fuels, food, and chemicals in batteries. It is released during chemical reactions, e.g. as heat when a fuel burns, when the **electromagnetic potential energy** of the atoms and molecules changes.

* **Acceleration due to gravity**, 18. **Compression**, 7. **Electromagnetic force**, **Force field**, **Gravitational force**, 6. **Intermolecular forces**, 7. **SI units**, 96. **Tension**, 7.

- **Nuclear potential energy**. The **potential energy** stored in an atomic **nucleus***. It is released during **radioactive decay***.

- **Kinetic energy (K.E.)**. The energy associated with movement. It takes the form of **translational**, **rotational** and **vibrational energy**.

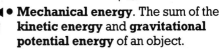

$$K.E. = \frac{1}{2}mv^2$$

where m = mass;
v = velocity.

Kinetic energy of two objects linked by spring

Translational

Vibrational

Rotational

◄ • **Mechanical energy**. The sum of the **kinetic energy** and **gravitational potential energy** of an object.

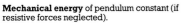

Mechanical energy of pendulum constant (if resistive forces neglected).

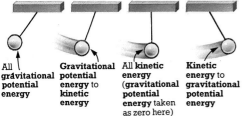

| All gravitational potential energy | Gravitational potential energy to kinetic energy | All kinetic energy (gravitational potential energy taken as zero here) | Kinetic energy to gravitational potential energy |

- **Internal** or **thermal energy**. The sum of the **kinetic energy** and the **molecular potential energy** of the molecules in an object. If the temperature of an object increases, so does its internal energy.

▼

- **Heat energy** or **heat**. The energy which flows from one place to another because of a difference in temperature (see pages 28-33). When heat energy is absorbed by an object, its **internal energy** increases.

- **Wave energy**. The energy associated with wave action. For example, the energy of a water wave consists of the **gravitational potential energy** and **kinetic energy** of the water molecules.

- **Electric** and **magnetic energy**. The types of energy associated with electric charge and moving electric charge (current). They are collectively referred to as **electromagnetic energy**.

- **Radiation**. Any energy in the form of **electromagnetic waves*** or streams of particles. See also pages 28 and 86-87.

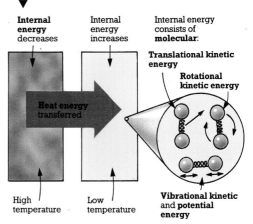

Internal energy decreases

Internal energy increases

Internal energy consists of **molecular**:

Translational kinetic energy

Rotational kinetic energy

Heat energy transferred

High temperature

Low temperature

Vibrational kinetic and **potential energy**

- **Power**. The rate of doing work or the rate of change of energy. The **SI unit*** of power is the **watt (W)**, which is equal to 1 joule per second.

▼

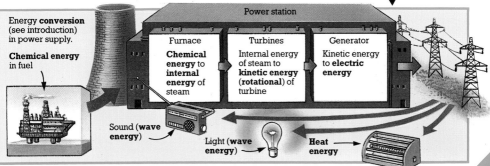

Energy **conversion** (see introduction) in power supply.

Chemical energy in fuel

Power station

| Furnace | Turbines | Generator |
| **Chemical energy** to **internal energy** of steam | Internal energy of steam to **kinetic energy (rotational)** of turbine | Kinetic energy to **electric energy** |

Sound (**wave energy**)

Light (**wave energy**)

Heat energy

* **Electromagnetic waves**, 44; **Nucleus**, 82; **Radioactive decay**, 87; **SI units**, 96.

9

Motion

Motion is the change in position and orientation of an object. The motion of a **rigid** object (one which does not change shape) is made up of **translational motion**, or **translation**, i.e. movement of the **centre of mass** from one place to another and **rotational motion**, or **rotation**, i.e. movement around its centre of mass. The study of the motion of points is called **kinematics**.

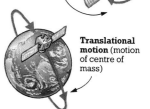

Satellite spinning in orbit

Rotational motion (motion around **centre of mass**)

Translational motion (motion of centre of mass)

Linear motion

Linear or **rectilinear motion** is movement in a straight line and is the simplest form of **translational motion** (see introduction). The linear motion of any rigid object is described as the motion of its **centre of mass**.

- **Centre of mass**. The point which acts as though the total mass of the object were at that point. The centre of mass of a **rigid** object (see introduction) is in the same position as its **centre of gravity** (the point through which the earth's gravitational force acts on the object).

Centre of mass of uniform disc is in centre.

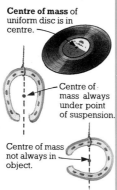

Centre of mass always under point of suspension.

Centre of mass not always in object.

- **Displacement**. The distance and direction of an object from a fixed reference point. It is a **vector quantity***. The position of an object can be expressed by its displacement from a specified point.

Reference point

Displacement of yacht = 200 m north

Direction   Distance

- **Speed**. The distance an object travels in a certain length of time. If the speed of an object is constant, it is said to be moving with **uniform speed**. The **average speed** of an object over a time interval is the distance travelled by the object divided by the time interval. The **instantaneous speed** is the speed at any moment.

Train travels from A to C (100 km) in two hours, stopping at B.

Instantaneous speed at B = 0

$$\text{Average speed} = \frac{100\text{ km}}{2\text{ hrs}}$$

$$= 50\text{ km h}^{-1}$$

- **Velocity**. The **speed** and direction of an object (i.e. its **displacement** in a given time). It is a **vector quantity***. **Uniform velocity**, **average velocity** and **instantaneous velocity** are all defined in a similar way to **uniform speed** etc. (see speed).

Graph of **displacement** against time

Displacement

Velocity here equal to gradient ds/dt

ds

dt

At t = 0, gradient = 0 so velocity = 0

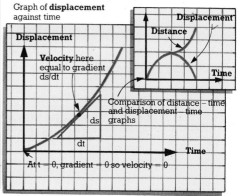

Displacement

Distance

Time

Comparison of distance – time and displacement – time graphs

Time

*Vector quantity, 105.

• **Relative velocity**. The **velocity** which an object appears to have when seen by an observer who may be moving. This is known as the velocity of the object relative to the observer.

40 m s⁻¹ — 40 m s^{-1}

Relative velocity of B (seen from A) = 70 m s⁻¹ to left.

30 m s^{-1}

Relative velocity of A (seen from B) = 70 m s⁻¹ to right.

• **Acceleration**. The change of **velocity** of an object in a certain time. It is a **vector quantity***. An object accelerates if its **speed** changes (the usual case in **linear motion**) or its direction of travel changes (the usual case in **circular motion***). **Deceleration** in one direction is acceleration in the opposite direction to the motion (negative acceleration). An object whose velocity is changing the same amount in equal amounts of time is moving with **uniform acceleration**.

$$v = u + at$$
$$s = \tfrac{1}{2}(u + v)t$$
$$s = ut + \tfrac{1}{2}at^2$$
$$v^2 = u^2 + 2as$$

where t = time; u = initial **velocity** at time = 0; v = final velocity after t; s = displacement after t; a = acceleration (constant).

• **Equations of uniformly accelerated motion**. Equations which are used in calculations involving **linear motion** with **uniform acceleration**. A **sign convention** must be used. The equations use **displacement**, not distance, so changes of direction must be considered.

Graphs of **velocity** against time

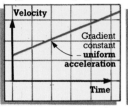

Velocity

Gradient constant – **uniform acceleration**

Time

Distance travelled in equal time intervals increases.

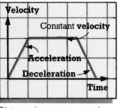

Velocity

Constant **velocity**

Acceleration

Deceleration

Time

Distance increases, remains constant, then decreases.

Sign convention   Right chosen as positive

$- \longleftarrow | \longrightarrow +$

Displacement 0

Negative displacement ←   → Positive displacement

Object moving to left has negative **velocity**. ←   → Object moving to right has positive velocity.

Velocity becoming more positive means positive **acceleration**. ←   → Velocity becoming more negative means negative acceleration (**deceleration**).

Rotational motion

Rotational motion is the movement of an object about its **centre of mass**. In rotational motion, each part of the object moves along a different path, so that the object cannot be considered as a whole in calculations. It must be split into small pieces and the **circular motion*** of each piece must be considered separately. From this, the overall motion of the object can be seen.

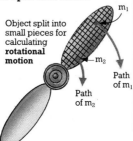

Object split into small pieces for calculating **rotational motion**

m_1

m_2

Path of m_1

Path of m_2

• **Sign convention**. A method used to distinguish between motion in opposite directions. One direction is chosen as positive, and the other is then negative. The sign convention must be used when using the equations of motion (see above).

* Circular motion, 17;
Vector quantity, 108.

Dynamics

Dynamics is the study of the relationship between the motion of an object and the forces acting on it. A single force on an object causes it to change speed and/or direction (i.e. **accelerate***). If two or more forces act and there is no resultant force, the object does not accelerate, but changes shape.

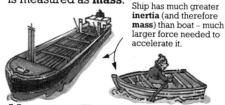

Two equal but opposite forces. No resultant force – no acceleration, but rope stretches.

Forces not equal. Rope still stretches, but also accelerates to left due to resultant force.

- **Newton's laws of motion**. Three laws formulated by Newton in the late 1770's which relate force and motion.

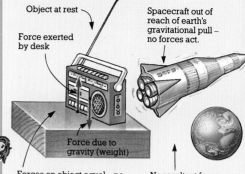

Object at rest

Force exerted by desk

Spacecraft out of reach of earth's gravitational pull – no forces act.

Force due to gravity (weight)

Forces on object equal – no resultant force, hence no acceleration.

No resultant force – constant velocity

- **Newton's first law**. If an object is at rest, or if its speed and direction are constant, then the resultant force on it is zero.

- **Mass**. A measurement of the **inertia** of an object. The force needed to accelerate an object by a given amount depends on its mass – a larger mass needs a larger force.

- **Inertia**. The tendency of an object to resist a change of velocity (i.e. to resist a force trying to accelerate it). It is measured as **mass**.

Ship has much greater **inertia** (and therefore **mass**) than boat – much larger force needed to accelerate it.

- **Momentum**. The **mass** of an object multiplied by its velocity. Since velocity is a **vector quantity***, so is momentum. See also **law of conservation of linear momentum**.

v

m

$$\text{Momentum} = mv$$

where m = mass; v = velocity.

- **Impulse**. The force acting on an object multiplied by the time for which the force acts. From **Newton's second law**, impulse is equal to the change in **momentum** of an object. An equal change in momentum can be achieved by a small force for a long time or a large force for a short time.

"Crumple zone" increases **collision** time – force is smaller.

$$\text{Impulse} = Ft$$

where F = force; t = time.

Since force is rate of change of momentum (see **Newton's second law**) then:

$$\text{Impulse} = \frac{\text{change in momentum}}{}$$

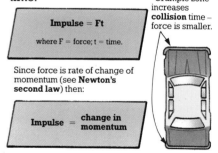

- **Collision**. An occurrence which results in two or more objects exerting forces on each other. This is not the everyday idea of a collision, because the objects do not necessarily have to be in contact.

* Acceleration, 11; Vector quantity, 108.

- **Newton's second law**. If the **momentum** of an object changes, i.e. if it accelerates, then there must be a resultant force acting on it. Normally, the **mass** of the object is constant, and the force is thus proportional to the acceleration of the object. The direction of the acceleration is the same as the direction of the force.

$$\text{Force} = \frac{\text{change in momentum}}{\text{time}}$$

If **mass** remains constant (as here), then:

$$\text{Force} = \text{mass} \times \text{acceleration}$$

Example: tennis ball (mass 0.05 kg) hit by racket undergoes change of **momentum**. Resultant force found as follows:

Note movement to right considered as positive (see **sign convention**, page 11).

Velocity −10 m s^{-1} (i.e. to left)

At impact:

Time of impact with racket = 0.01 s

After impact, velocity = 20 m s^{-1}

$$\text{Force} = \frac{\text{change in momentum}}{\text{time}} = \frac{(0.05 \times 20) - (0.05 \times -10)}{0.01} = 150 \text{ N}$$

$$\text{Force} = \text{mass} \times \text{acceleration} = \frac{\text{mass} \times \text{change in velocity}}{\text{time}}$$

$$= \frac{0.05 \times 30}{0.01} = 150 \text{ N}$$

Racket exerts force on ball, accelerating it in opposite direction.

Ball exerts equal and opposite force on racket (felt as sudden slowing down of racket).

◄ - **Newton's third law**. Forces always occur in equal and opposite pairs called the **action** and **reaction**. Thus if object A exerts a force on object B, object B exerts an equal but opposite force on A. These forces do not cancel each other out, as they act on different objects.

- **Law of conservation of linear momentum**. When two or more objects exert forces on each other (are in **collision**), their total **momentum** remains constant, provided no external forces act. If the time for the collision is very small and the system is considered just before and just after the collision, forces such as friction can be ignored.

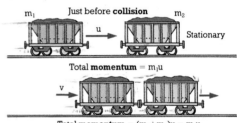

Just before **collision**

m_1　　　m_2　Stationary

Total **momentum** $= m_1 u$

v

Total **momentum** $= (m_1 + m_2)v = m_1 u$

Mass increases – velocity decreases to conserve momentum.

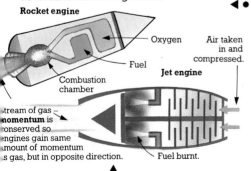

Rocket engine

Oxygen

Fuel

Combustion chamber

Stream of gas momentum is conserved so engines gain same amount of momentum as gas, but in opposite direction.

Air taken in and compressed.

Jet engine

Fuel burnt.

◄ - **Rocket engine**. An engine which produces a high velocity stream of gas through a nozzle by burning fuel held on board. The **mass** of gas is small, but its high velocity means it has a high **momentum**. The rocket gains an equal amount of momentum in the opposite direction (see **law of conservation of linear momentum**). Rocket engines are used in space because other engines require air.

- **Jet engine**. An engine in which air is drawn in at the front to burn fuel, producing a high velocity jet of gas. The principle is the same as that for the **rocket engine**, except that the gas is produced differently and the engine cannot be used in space because it requires air.

Turning forces

A single force produces an **acceleration*** (see **dynamics**, page 12). In **linear motion***, it is a **linear acceleration**. In **rotational motion***, **angular acceleration*** (spinning faster or slower) is caused by a turning force or **moment** acting away from the axis of rotation (the **fulcrum**).

- **Moment** or **torque**. A measure of the ability of a force to rotate an object about an axis (the **fulcrum**). It is the size of the force multiplied by the perpendicular distance from the axis to the line along which the force acts (see diagram, right). The **SI unit*** of moment is the **Newton metre (N m)**.

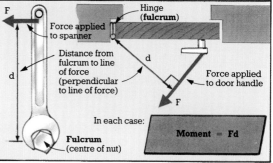

Force applied to spanner
Hinge (**fulcrum**)
Distance from fulcrum to line of force (perpendicular to line of force)
Force applied to door handle
In each case:
$$\text{Moment} = Fd$$
Fulcrum (centre of nut)

Balanced weighing machine in **rotational equilibrium**

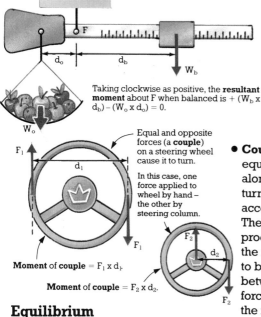

Taking clockwise as positive, the **resultant moment** about F when balanced is $+ (W_b \times d_b) - (W_o \times d_o) = 0$.

Equal and opposite forces (a **couple**) on a steering wheel cause it to turn.

In this case, one force applied to wheel by hand – the other by steering column.

Moment of couple $= F_1 \times d_1$.

Moment of couple $= F_2 \times d_2$.

Equilibrium

When an object is not accelerating, then the resultant force (the combined effect of all the forces acting on it) is zero and it is said to be in **equilibrium**. It can be in **linear equilibrium** (i.e. the **centre of mass***

When considering moments, the axis about which they are taken must be stated and a **sign convention*** must be used to distinguish between clockwise and anti-clockwise moments. The **resultant moment** is the single moment which has the same effect as all the individual moments acting.

- **Couple**. Two parallel forces which are equal and opposite but do not act along the same line. They produce a turning effect only, with no resultant acceleration of the **centre of mass***. The **resultant moment** (see above) produced by a couple is the sum of the moments produced and works out to be the perpendicular distance between the lines along which the forces act, multiplied by the size of the forces.

is not accelerating) and/or **rotational equilibrium** (i.e. not accelerating about the centre of mass). In addition, both cases of equilibrium are either **static** (not moving) or **dynamic** (moving).

* **Acceleration**, 11; **Angular acceleration**, 17; **Centre of mass**, Linear motion, 10; **Rotational motion**, **Sign convention**, 11; **SI units**, 96.

- **Linear equilibrium**. The state of an object when there is no acceleration of its **centre of mass***, i.e. its speed and direction of motion do not change. The resultant force on the object when it is in linear equilibrium must be zero (see also **Newton's third law**, page 13).

Aircraft in flight in **dynamic linear equilibrium** and **static rotational equilibrium** – constant speed in straight line

$L = W$ and $D = T$
No resultant force

Lift L
Drag* D   Thrust T
Weight W

Aircraft on ground in **static equilibrium** (**linear** and **rotational**)

Force of ground on aircraft (through wheels) R
$W = R$
Weight W

- **Rotational equilibrium**. The state of an object when there is no **angular acceleration***, i.e. it spins at constant **angular velocity***. If an object is in rotational equilibrium, the **resultant moment** (see **moment**) about any axis is zero. This is known as the **principle of moments**.

|← 1 m →|← 2 m →|

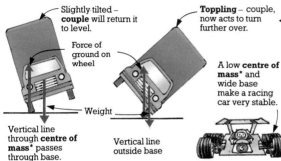

800 N   400 N

Beam in **static rotational equilibrium**, since 800 x 1 = 400 x 2

Slightly tilted – **couple** will return it to level.

Force of ground on wheel

Weight

Vertical line through **centre of mass*** passes through base.

Vertical line outside base

Toppling – couple, now acts to turn further over.

A low **centre of mass*** and wide base make a racing car very stable.

◄ ● **Toppling**. A condition which occurs if the vertical line through the **centre of mass*** of an object does not pass through the base of the object. If this occurs, a **couple** of the weight and reaction rotates the object further over (see diagram, left).

- **Stable equilibrium**. A state in which an object moved a small distance from its equilibrium position returns to that position. This happens if the **centre of mass*** is raised when the object is moved.

- **Unstable equilibrium**. A state in which an object moved a small distance from its equilibrium position moves further from that position. This happens if the **centre of mass*** is lowered when the object is moved.

- **Neutral equilibrium**. A state in which an object moved a small distance from its equilibrium position remains in the new position. This happens if the **centre of mass*** remains at the same height.

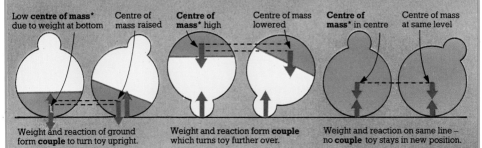

Low **centre of mass*** due to weight at bottom

Centre of mass raised

Centre of mass* high

Centre of mass lowered

Centre of mass* in centre

Centre of mass at same level

Weight and reaction of ground form **couple** to turn toy upright.

Weight and reaction form **couple** which turns toy further over.

Weight and reaction on same line – no **couple** toy stays in new position.

* **Angular acceleration, Angular velocity**, 17; **Centre of mass**, 10; **Drag**, 19 (**Terminal velocity**).

15

Periodic motion

Periodic motion is any motion which repeats itself exactly at regular intervals. Examples of periodic motion are objects moving in a circle (**circular motion**), the swing of a pendulum and the vibration of molecules. **Wave motion*** consists of the periodic motion of particles or fields.

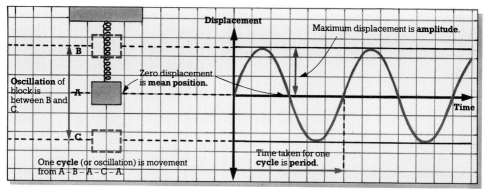

Maximum displacement is **amplitude**.

Zero displacement is **mean position**.

Oscillation of block is between B and C.

One **cycle** (or oscillation) is movement from A – B – A – C – A.

Time taken for one cycle is **period**.

- **Cycle**. The movement between a point during a motion and the same point when the motion repeats. For example, one rotation of a spinning object.

- **Oscillation**. Periodic motion between two extremes, e.g. a mass moving up and down on the end of a spring. In an oscillating system, there is a continuous change between **kinetic energy*** and **potential energy***. The total energy of a system (sum of its kinetic and potential energy) remains constant if there is no **damping**.

- **Period (T)**. The time taken to complete one **cycle** of a motion, e.g. the period of rotation of the earth about its axis is 24 hours.

- **Frequency (f)**. The number of **cycles** of a particular motion in one second. The **SI unit*** of frequency is the **Hertz (Hz)**, which is equal to one cycle per second.

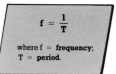

$$f = \frac{1}{T}$$

where f = **frequency**; T = **period**.

- **Mean position**. The position about which an object **oscillates**, and at which it comes to rest after oscillating, e.g. the mean position of a pendulum is when it is vertical. The position of zero displacement of an oscillating particle is usually taken as this point.

- **Amplitude**. The maximum displacement of an **oscillating** particle from its **mean position**.

- **Damping**. The process whereby **oscillations** die down due to a loss of energy, e.g. shock absorbers in cars cause oscillations to die down after a car has gone over a bump.

Damping in an **oscillating** system

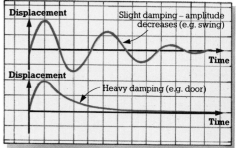

Slight damping – amplitude decreases (e.g. swing)

Heavy damping (e.g. door)

* **Kinetic energy**, 9; **Potential energy**, 8; **SI units**, 96; **Wave motion**, 34.

Natural or **free oscillation**. The **oscillation** of a system when left after being given a start. The **period** and **frequency** of the system are called the **natural period** and **natural frequency** (these remain the same as long as the **damping** is not too great).

Natural oscillation

Swings at natural frequency after being released.

Forced oscillation. The **oscillation** of a system when given a repeated driving force (a force applied to the system) at regular intervals. The system is made to oscillate at the **frequency** of the driving force, irrespective of its **natural frequency**.

Forced oscillation. Driving force is person pushing at bottom of swing.

Frequency is that of pushing person – amplitude constant and small.

Resonance. The effect exhibited by a system in which the **frequency** of the driving force (a force applied to the system) is about the same as the **natural frequency** of the system. The system then has a large **amplitude**.

Driving force at end of each swing – at **natural frequency** of swing.

Amplitude increases – resonance occurs.

Circular motion

Speed round circle constant.

Object takes time t to move through angle θ.

Angular velocity is a measure of the angle moved through per second. It is measured in radians per second.

$$\text{Angular velocity} = \theta/t \text{ rad s}^{-1}$$

Angular acceleration involves a change in angular velocity (i.e. speed round circle changes).

Constant speed

Velocity at A

Direction of **centripetal acceleration** (and **centripetal force**)

$$a = \frac{v^2}{r}$$

where a = **centripetal acceleration**; v = velocity around circle; r = radius of circle.

Velocity at B

Uniform circular motion is the motion of an object in a circle at constant speed. Since the direction (and therefore the velocity) changes, the object is constantly accelerating towards the centre (**centripetal acceleration**), and so there is a force acting towards the centre. Circular motion can be considered in terms of **angular velocity**.

- **Centripetal acceleration** (**a**). The acceleration of an object in circular motion (see above) acting towards the centre of the circle.

- **Centripetal force**. The force which acts on an object towards the centre of a circle to produce **centripetal acceleration**, and so keeps the object moving in a circle.

Centripetal force to move person in circle applied by seat.

- **Centrifugal force**. The equal and opposite reaction (see **Newton's second law**, page 13) to the **centripetal force**. Note that it does not act on the object moving in the circle and is not considered.

Reaction to centripetal force (**centrifugal force**)

17

Gravitation

Gravitation is the effect of the **gravitational force*** of attraction (see also page 104) which acts between all objects in the universe. It is noticed with massive objects like the planets, which remain in orbit because of it. The gravitational force between an object and a planet, which pulls the object downwards, is called the **weight** of the object.

- **Newton's law of gravitation.** States that there is a gravitational force of attraction between any two objects with mass which depends on their masses and the distance between them. The **gravitational constant (G)** has a value of 6.7×10^{-11} N m^2 kg^{-2}, and its small value means that gravitational forces are negligible unless one of the masses is very large.

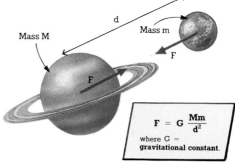

Mass M   d   Mass m   F   F

$$F = G \frac{Mm}{d^2}$$

where G = gravitational constant.

- **Weight.** The gravitational pull of a massive object (e.g. a planet) on another object. The weight of an object is not constant, but depends on the distance from, and mass of the planet. Hence, although the mass of an object is independent of its position, its weight is not.

- **Acceleration due to gravity (g).** The **acceleration*** produced by the gravitational force of attraction. Its value is the same for any mass at a given place. It is about 9.8 m s^{-2} on the earth's surface, and decreases above the surface according to **Newton's law of gravitation**. The value of 9.8 m s^{-2} is used as a unit of acceleration (the **g-force**).

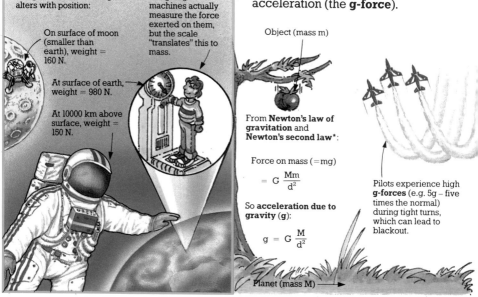

Weight of mass of 100 kg alters with position:

On surface of moon (smaller than earth), weight = 160 N.

At surface of earth, weight = 980 N.

At 10000 km above surface, weight = 150 N.

Weighing machines actually measure the force exerted on them, but the scale "translates" this to mass.

Object (mass m)

From **Newton's law of gravitation** and **Newton's second law***:

Force on mass (=mg)

$$= G \frac{Mm}{d^2}$$

So **acceleration due to gravity (g)**:

$$g = G \frac{M}{d^2}$$

Planet (mass M)

Pilots experience high **g-forces** (e.g. 5g – five times the normal) during tight turns, which can lead to blackout.

* Acceleration, 11; **Gravitational force**, 6; **Newton's second law**, 13.

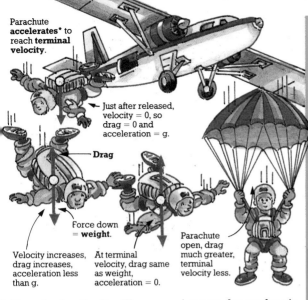

Parachute **accelerates*** to reach **terminal velocity**.

Just after released, velocity = 0, so drag = 0 and acceleration = g.

Drag

Force down = **weight**.

Velocity increases, drag increases, acceleration less than g.

At terminal velocity, drag same as weight, acceleration = 0.

Parachute open, drag much greater, terminal velocity less.

- **Weightlessness**. The state in which an object does not exert any force on its surroundings.

- **True weightlessness**. **Weightlessness** due to an object being in a gravity-free region.

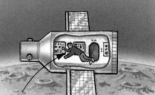

Astronaut **free falls** in same way as spacecraft and is therefore **apparently weightless** inside the craft.

- **Terminal velocity**. The maximum, constant velocity reached by an object falling through a gas or liquid. As the velocity increases, the resistance due to the air or liquid (**drag**) increases. Eventually, the drag becomes equal to the **weight** of the object.

- **Apparent weightlessness**. The state of an object when it is as if there were no gravitational forces acting. This occurs if two objects **accelerate*** independently in the same way.

- **Escape velocity**. The minimum velocity at which an object must travel in order to escape the gravitational pull of a planet without further propulsion. It is about 40000 km h^{-1} on earth.

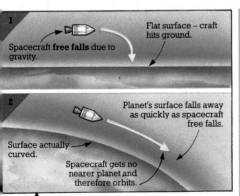

1 Spacecraft **free falls** due to gravity.

Flat surface – craft hits ground.

2 Planet's surface falls away as quickly as spacecraft free falls.

Surface actually curved.

Spacecraft gets no nearer planet and therefore orbits.

- **Geo-stationary** or **parking orbit**. The path of a satellite which orbits the earth in the same direction as the rotation of the earth so that it stays above the same place on the surface all the time. The satellite is said to have a **period*** of 24 hours.

Satellite in **geo-stationary orbit** above point P

Communications sent between points in this area by bouncing them off the satellite.

- **Free fall**. The unrestricted motion of an object when it is acted upon only by the gravitational force (i.e. when there are no resistive or other forces acting, e.g. air resistance).

P

Machines

A **machine** is a device which is used to overcome a force called the **load**. This force is applied at one point and the machine works by the application of another force called the **effort** at a different point. For example, a small effort exerted on the rope of a **pulley** overcomes the weight of the object being raised by the pulley.

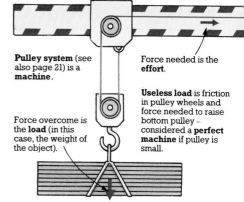

Pulley system (see also page 21) is a **machine**.

Force needed is the **effort**.

Useless load is friction in pulley wheels and force needed to raise bottom pulley – considered a **perfect machine** if pulley is small.

Force overcome is the **load** (in this case, the weight of the object).

- **Perfect machine**. A theoretical machine, with a **useless load** of zero. Machines in which the useless load is negligible compared to the load can be considered as perfect machines.

- **Useless load**. The force needed to overcome the **frictional forces*** between the moving parts of a machine and to raise any of its moving parts.

- **Mechanical advantage (M.A.).** The load divided by the effort. A mechanical advantage greater than one means that the load overcome is greater than the effort. The mechanical advantage of a **perfect machine** is always the same; that of any given real machine increases slightly with load because **useless load** becomes negligible as load increases.

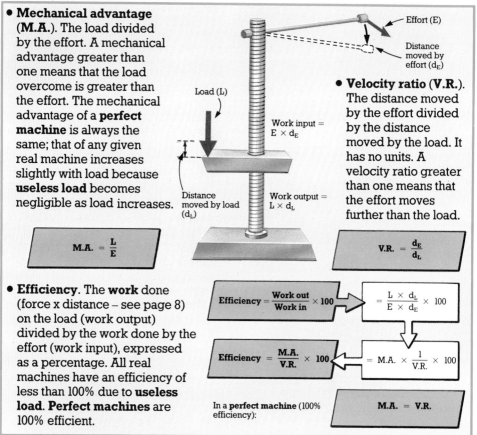

Load (L)

Work input = $E \times d_E$

Effort (E)

Distance moved by effort (d_E)

- **Velocity ratio (V.R.).** The distance moved by the effort divided by the distance moved by the load. It has no units. A velocity ratio greater than one means that the effort moves further than the load.

Distance moved by load (d_L)

Work output = $L \times d_L$

$$\text{M.A.} = \frac{L}{E}$$

$$\text{V.R.} = \frac{d_E}{d_L}$$

- **Efficiency**. The **work** done (force x distance – see page 8) on the load (work output) divided by the work done by the effort (work input), expressed as a percentage. All real machines have an efficiency of less than 100% due to **useless load**. **Perfect machines** are 100% efficient.

$$\text{Efficiency} = \frac{\text{Work out}}{\text{Work in}} \times 100$$

$$= \frac{L \times d_L}{E \times d_E} \times 100$$

$$\text{Efficiency} = \frac{\text{M.A.}}{\text{V.R.}} \times 100$$

$$= \text{M.A.} \times \frac{1}{\text{V.R.}} \times 100$$

In a **perfect machine** (100% efficiency):

$$\text{M.A.} = \text{V.R.}$$

* Frictional force, 7.

Examples of machines

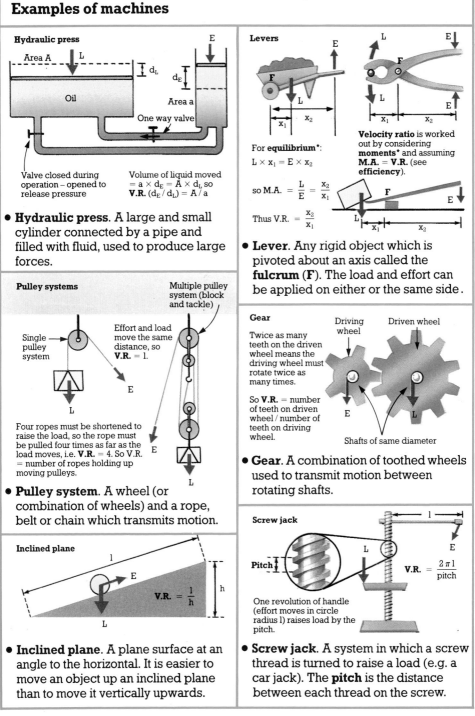

Hydraulic press

Area A · L · E · d_L · d_E · Oil · Area a · One way valve

Valve closed during operation – opened to release pressure

Volume of liquid moved $= a \times d_E = A \times d_L$ so
V.R. $(d_E / d_L) = A / a$

- **Hydraulic press**. A large and small cylinder connected by a pipe and filled with fluid, used to produce large forces.

Pulley systems

Multiple pulley system (block and tackle)

Single pulley system · E · L

Effort and load move the same distance, so **V.R.** = 1.

Four ropes must be shortened to raise the load, so the rope must be pulled four times as far as the load moves, i.e. **V.R.** = 4. So V.R. = number of ropes holding up moving pulleys.

- **Pulley system**. A wheel (or combination of wheels) and a rope, belt or chain which transmits motion.

Inclined plane

l · E · L · h · **V.R.** $= \dfrac{l}{h}$

- **Inclined plane**. A plane surface at an angle to the horizontal. It is easier to move an object up an inclined plane than to move it vertically upwards.

Levers

E · L · F · L · E

For **equilibrium**[*]:

$L \times x_1 = E \times x_2$

so M.A. $= \dfrac{L}{E} = \dfrac{x_2}{x_1}$

Thus V.R. $= \dfrac{x_2}{x_1}$

Velocity ratio is worked out by considering **moments**[*] and assuming **M.A.** = **V.R.** (see efficiency).

- **Lever**. Any rigid object which is pivoted about an axis called the **fulcrum (F)**. The load and effort can be applied on either or the same side.

Gear

Driving wheel · Driven wheel

Twice as many teeth on the driven wheel means the driving wheel must rotate twice as many times.

So **V.R.** = number of teeth on driven wheel / number of teeth on driving wheel.

E · L · Shafts of same diameter

- **Gear**. A combination of toothed wheels used to transmit motion between rotating shafts.

Screw jack

l · L · E · Pitch · **V.R.** $= \dfrac{2\pi l}{\text{pitch}}$

One revolution of handle (effort moves in circle radius l) raises load by the pitch.

- **Screw jack**. A system in which a screw thread is turned to raise a load (e.g. a car jack). The **pitch** is the distance between each thread on the screw.

Molecular properties

There are a number of properties of matter which can be explained in terms of the behaviour of molecules, in particular their behaviour due to the action of the forces between them (**intermolecular forces***). Among these properties, and explained below, are **elasticity**, **surface tension** and **viscosity**. See also pages 4-5 and 24-25.

Balloon is **elastic** (returns to original shape after stretching).

Cool wax is **plastic** (seal leaves permanent impression).

• **Elasticity**. The ability of a material to return to its original shape and size after distorting forces (i.e. **tension*** or **compression***) have been removed. Materials which have this ability are **elastic**; those which do not are **plastic**. Elasticity is a result of **intermolecular forces*** – if an object is stretched or compressed, its molecules move further apart or closer together respectively. This results in a force of attraction (in the first case) or repulsion (in the second), so the molecules return to their average separation when the distorting force is removed. This always happens while the strength of the force is below a certain level (different for each material), but all elastic materials finally become plastic if it exceeds this level (see **elastic limit** and **yield point**).

• **Hooke's law**. States that, when distorting forces are applied to an object, the **strain** is proportional to the **stress** (see diagram below). As the strength of the force increases, though, the **limit of proportionality** (or **proportional limit**) is reached, after which Hooke's law is no longer true (see graph, page 23).

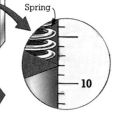

Spring balance uses **Hooke's law** to measure force. Spring is extended in proportion to force applied.

Stress divided by **strain** (see below left) is always same figure for a given material (**Young's modulus** – see page 114) until **limit of proportionality** is reached.

Scale **calibrated*** so that length of spring gives size of force in **newtons***.

Spring

10

1 kg

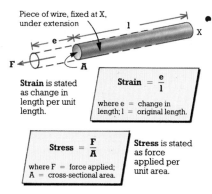

Piece of wire, fixed at X, under extension

l

e

X

F

A

Strain is stated as change in length per unit length.

$$Strain = \frac{e}{l}$$

where e = change in length; l = original length.

$$Stress = \frac{F}{A}$$

where F = force applied; A = cross-sectional area.

Stress is stated as force applied per unit area.

• **Elastic limit**. The point, just after the **limit of proportionality** (see **Hooke's law**), beyond which an object ceases to be **elastic**, in the sense that it does not return to its original shape and size when the distorting force is removed. It does return to a similar shape and size, but has suffered a permanent strain (it will continue to return to this new form if forces are applied, i.e. it stays elastic in this sense). The **yield stress** of a material is the value of the **stress** at its elastic limit. See graph, page 23.

  * **Calibration**, 115; **Compression, Intermolecular forces**, 7; **Newton**, 6; **Tension**, 7

- **Yield point**. The point, just after the **elastic limit**, at which a distorting force causes a major change in a material. In a **ductile** material, the internal structure changes – bonds between molecular layers break and the layers flow over each other. This change is called **plastic deformation**

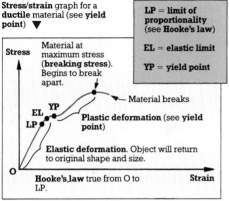

Stress/strain graph for a **ductile** material (see **yield point**) ▼

LP = limit of proportionality (see **Hooke's law**)

EL = elastic limit

YP = yield point

Stress

Material at maximum stress (**breaking stress**). Begins to break apart.

Material breaks

EL YP
LP

Plastic deformation (see **yield point**)

Elastic deformation. Object will return to original shape and size.

O

Hooke's law true from O to LP.

Strain

(the material becomes **plastic**). It continues as the force increases, and the material will eventually break. A **brittle** material, by contrast, will break at the yield point. The **yield value** of a material is the value of the **stress** at its yield point.

- **Viscosity**. The ease of flow of a fluid. It depends on the strength of the **frictional force*** between different layers of molecules as they slide over each other.

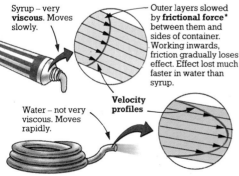

Syrup – very **viscous**. Moves slowly.

Outer layers slowed by **frictional force*** between them and sides of container. Working inwards, friction gradually loses effect. Effect lost much faster in water than syrup.

Velocity profiles

Water – not very viscous. Moves rapidly.

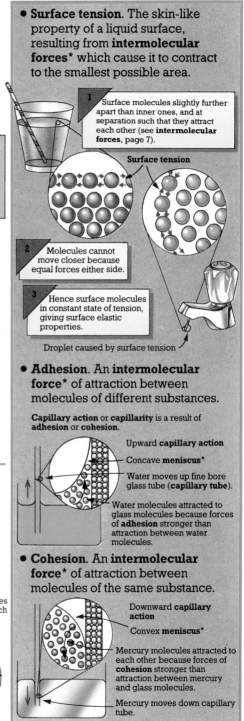

- **Surface tension**. The skin-like property of a liquid surface, resulting from **intermolecular forces*** which cause it to contract to the smallest possible area.

1 Surface molecules slightly further apart than inner ones, and at separation such that they attract each other (see **intermolecular forces**, page 7).

Surface tension

2 Molecules cannot move closer because equal forces either side.

3 Hence surface molecules in constant state of tension, giving surface elastic properties.

Droplet caused by surface tension

- **Adhesion**. An **intermolecular force*** of attraction between molecules of different substances.

Capillary action or **capillarity** is a result of **adhesion** or **cohesion**.

Upward **capillary action**

Concave **meniscus***

Water moves up fine bore glass tube (**capillary tube**).

Water molecules attracted to glass molecules because forces of **adhesion** stronger than attraction between water molecules.

- **Cohesion**. An **intermolecular force*** of attraction between molecules of the same substance.

Downward **capillary action**

Convex **meniscus***

Mercury molecules attracted to each other because forces of **cohesion** stronger than attraction between mercury and glass molecules.

Mercury moves down capillary tube.

* **Frictional force**, **Intermolecular forces**, 7, **Meniscus**, 115

Density

The **density** (ρ) of an object depends on both the mass of its molecules and its volume (see formula, right). For example, if one substance has a higher density than another, then the same volumes of the substances have different masses (the first greater than the second). Similarly, the same masses have different volumes.

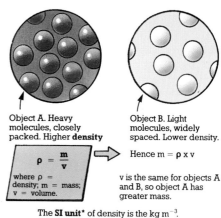

Object A. Heavy molecules, closely packed. Higher **density**.

Object B. Light molecules, widely spaced. Lower density.

$$\rho = \frac{m}{v}$$

where ρ = density; m = mass; v = volume.

Hence m = ρ x v

v is the same for objects A and B, so object A has greater mass.

The **SI unit*** of density is the kg m^{-3}.

- **Relative density** or **specific gravity**. The density of a substance relative to the density of water (which is 1000 kg m^{-3}). It indicates how much more or less dense than water a substance is, so the figures need no units, e.g. 1.5 (one and a half times as dense). It is found by dividing the mass of any volume of a substance by the mass of an equal volume of water.

- **Density bottle**. A container which, when completely full, holds a precisely measured volume of liquid (at constant temperature). It is used to measure the density of liquids (by measuring the mass of the bottle and liquid, subtracting the mass of the bottle and dividing by the volume of liquid).

Density bottle

Fine bore tube (**capillary tube**) in glass stopper. Bottle filled, stopper inserted, excess liquid rises through tube and runs out – ensures same volume each time.

- **Eureka can**. A can used to measure the volume of a solid object with an irregular shape, in order to calculate its density. The volume of water displaced is equal to the volume of the object. The density of the object is its mass divided by this volume.

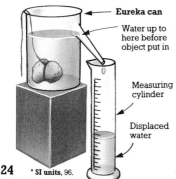

Eureka can

Water up to here before object put in

Measuring cylinder

Displaced water

Pressure

Pressure is the force, acting at right angles, exerted by a solid, liquid or gas on unit area of a substance (solid, liquid or gas).

The greater the force on a fixed area, the greater the pressure.

$$\text{Pressure} = \frac{\text{force}}{\text{area}}$$

The **SI unit*** pressure is th pascal (**Pa**).

The greater the area over which a fixed force acts, the lower the pressure.

Weight of air molecules above earth (force) creates **atmospheric pressure**. So the fewer there are (i.e. the higher the altitude), the lower the pressure.

Similarly, the more water molecules above a point, the greater the weight (force), so the greater the pressure.

Snow shoes increase area, weight (force) the same, so pressure decreases (feet do not sink into snow).

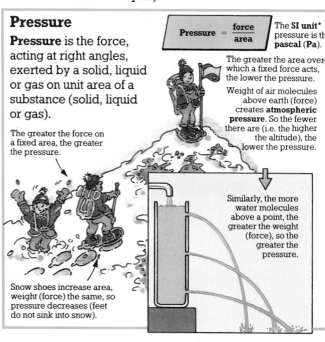

* SI units, 96.

Objects in fluids

An object in a fluid experiences an upward force called the **upthrust**. According to **Archimedes' principle**, this is equal to the weight of the fluid the object displaces. The **principle of flotation** further states that, if the object is floating, the weight of displaced fluid (upthrust) is equal to its own weight (floating here means stationary at any point in the fluid). It can be shown (see below) that whether an object sinks, rises or floats in a fluid depends entirely on density.

Calibration, 115.

Archimedes' principle

$$\text{Upthrust} = \frac{\text{weight of fluid}}{\text{displaced}}$$

Principle of flotation

For a floating object:
$$U = W$$
where U = upthrust; W = weight of object.

Weight = mass (m) x acceleration due to gravity (g)

Mass = density (ρ) x volume (v)

So weight (of object or fluid displaced) = ρvg

Submarines demonstrate two principles above right. Altering air/water mix in ballast tanks alters density (density of object made of more than one material is average density of different materials). See below.

Archimedes' principle says submarine has two forces acting on it – its own weight and the **upthrust**.

1. If $U = W$, sub floats (see **principle of flotation**).

2. If U becomes greater than W, sub starts to rise.

Both W and $U = \rho vg$ (see box, above). v and g are the same for both, and density (ρ) of water is constant. So 1,2 and 3 can be brought about by altering density of sub. In 1, it is the same as that of water, in 2 it is less and in 3 it is greater.

Sub breaks surface and floats. $U = W$, though density still less than that of water (see below), because now volume of water displaced is less.

3. If U becomes less than W, sub starts to sink.

● **Barometer.** An instrument used to measure **atmospheric pressure** (see picture, left). There are several common types.

Simple barometer
Torricellian vacuum (no pressure acting down)
Atmospheric pressure = 760 mm of mercury
Atmospheric pressure
Fixed diameter tube
Mercury

Manometer
Atmospheric pressure
Pressures at x_1 and x_2 (same level) must be the same
So pressure of gas = pressure at x_2
= atmospheric pressure + pressure of liquid h
Gas →
x_1
Gas pressure
Atmospheric pressure
h
x_2

● **Manometer.** A U-shaped tube containing a liquid. It is used to measure difference in fluid pressures.

● **Hydrometer** or **aerometer.** An instrument which measures the density of a liquid by the level at which it floats in that liquid. If the liquid is very dense, the hydrometer floats near the surface, as only a small volume of liquid need be displaced to equal the weight of the hydrometer.

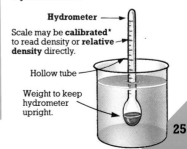

Hydrometer
Scale may be **calibrated** to read density or **relative density** directly.
Hollow tube
Weight to keep hydrometer upright.

25

Temperature

The **temperature** of an object is a measurement of how hot the object is. It is measured using **thermometers** which can be **calibrated*** to show a number of different temperature scales. The internationally accepted scales are the **absolute temperature scale** and the **Celsius scale**.

- **Thermometer**. An instrument used to measure temperature. There are many different types and they all work by measuring a property which changes with temperature – a **thermometric property**. **Liquid-in-glass thermometers**, for example, measure the volume of a liquid (they are **calibrated*** so that increases in volume mark rises in temperature).

- **Liquid-in-glass thermometer**. A common type of **thermometer** which measures temperature by the expansion of a liquid in a fine bore glass tube (**capillary tube**). A glass bulb holds a reservoir of the liquid, which is usually either mercury or coloured alcohol. These are very responsive to temperature change – mercury is used for higher temperature ranges and alcohol for lower ones.

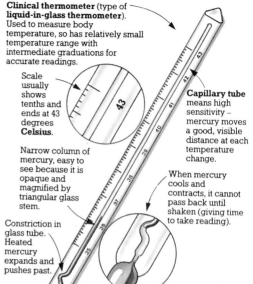

Clinical thermometer (type of liquid-in-glass thermometer). Used to measure body temperature, so has relatively small temperature range with intermediate graduations for accurate readings.

Scale usually shows tenths and ends at 43 degrees **Celsius**.

Narrow column of mercury, easy to see because it is opaque and magnified by triangular glass stem.

Constriction in glass tube. Heated mercury expands and pushes past.

Capillary tube means high sensitivity – mercury moves a good, visible distance at each temperature change.

When mercury cools and contracts, it cannot pass back until shaken (giving time to take reading).

Glass bulb is thin-walled so mercury heats up quickly.

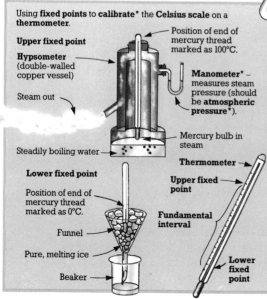

Using **fixed points** to **calibrate*** the Celsius scale on a thermometer.

Upper fixed point

Hypsometer (double-walled copper vessel)

Steam out

Steadily boiling water

Position of end of mercury thread marked as 100°C.

Manometer* – measures steam pressure (should be **atmospheric pressure***).

Mercury bulb in steam

Thermometer

Upper fixed point

Fundamental interval

Lower fixed point

Position of end of mercury thread marked as 0°C.

Funnel

Pure, melting ice

Beaker

Lower fixed point

- **Fixed point**. A temperature at which certain recognisable changes always take place (under given conditions), and which can thus be given a value against which all other temperatures can be measured. Examples are the **ice point** (the temperature at which pure ice melts) and the **steam point** (the temperature of steam above water boiling under **atmospheric pressure***). Two fixed points are used to **calibrate*** a thermometer – a **lower** and an **upper fixed point**. The distance between these points is the **fundamental interval**.

- **Maximum** and **minimum thermometers.** Special **liquid-in-glass thermometers** which record the maximum or minimum temperature reached over a period of time. They contain a metal and glass **index** (see picture) which is pushed up or pulled down (respectively) by the liquid **meniscus***. The index stays at the maximum or minimum position it reaches during the time the thermometer is left. It is reset using a magnet.

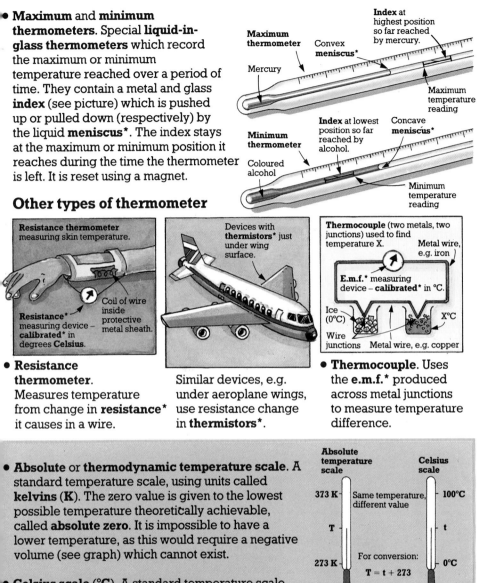

Maximum thermometer
Convex **meniscus***
Mercury
Index at highest position so far reached by mercury.
Maximum temperature reading

Minimum thermometer
Coloured alcohol
Index at lowest position so far reached by alcohol.
Concave **meniscus***
Minimum temperature reading

Other types of thermometer

Resistance thermometer measuring skin temperature.
Resistance* measuring device – **calibrated*** in degrees **Celsius**.
Coil of wire inside protective metal sheath.

Devices with **thermistors*** just under wing surface.

Thermocouple (two metals, two junctions) used to find temperature X.
Metal wire, e.g. iron
E.m.f.* measuring device – **calibrated*** in °C.
Ice (0°C)
X°C
Wire junctions
Metal wire, e.g. copper

- **Resistance thermometer.** Measures temperature from change in **resistance*** it causes in a wire.

Similar devices, e.g. under aeroplane wings, use resistance change in **thermistors***.

- **Thermocouple.** Uses the **e.m.f.*** produced across metal junctions to measure temperature difference.

- **Absolute** or **thermodynamic temperature scale.** A standard temperature scale, using units called **kelvins (K).** The zero value is given to the lowest possible temperature theoretically achievable, called **absolute zero.** It is impossible to have a lower temperature, as this would require a negative volume (see graph) which cannot exist.

- **Celsius scale (°C).** A standard temperature scale identical in graduations to the **absolute temperature scale,** but with the zero and one hundred degree values given to the **ice point** and **steam point** respectively (see **fixed point**).

- **Fahrenheit scale (°F).** An old scale with the values 32°F and 212°F given to the **ice point** and **steam point** respectively (see **fixed point**). It is rarely used in scientific work.

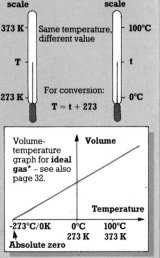

Absolute temperature scale
Celsius scale
373 K — Same temperature, different value — 100°C
T — t
273 K — For conversion: $T = t + 273$ — 0°C

Volume-temperature graph for **ideal gas*** – see also page 32.
Volume
Temperature
-273°C/0K
0°C / 273 K
100°C / 373 K
Absolute zero

*Calibration, 115; **Electromotive force (e.m.f.)**, 60; **Ideal gas**, 33; **Meniscus**, 115; **Resistance**, 62; **Thermistor**, 65.

Transfer of heat

Whenever there is a temperature difference, **heat energy** (see page 9) is transferred by **conduction**, **convection** or **radiation** from the hotter to the cooler place. This increases the **internal energy*** of the cooler atoms, raising their temperature, and decreases the energy of the hotter atoms, lowering theirs. It continues until the temperature is the same across the region – a state called **thermal equilibrium**.

- **Conduction** or **thermal conduction**. The way in which heat energy is transferred in solids (and also, to a much lesser extent, in liquids and gases). In good **conductors** the energy transfer is rapid, occurring mainly by the movement of free **electrons*** (electrons which can move about), although also by the vibration of atoms – see **insulators** (bad conductors).

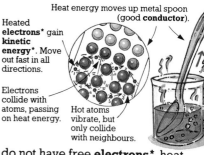

Heat energy moves up metal spoon (good **conductor**).

Heated **electrons*** gain **kinetic energy***. Move out fast in all directions.

Electrons collide with atoms, passing on heat energy.

Hot atoms vibrate, but only collide with neighbours.

- **Insulators**. Materials such as wood and most liquids and gases, in which the process of **conduction** is very slow (they are bad **conductors**). As they do not have free **electrons***, heat energy is only transferred by conduction by the vibration and collison of neighbouring atoms.

Temperature / **Distance**

Steeper **temperature gradient** means greater temperature difference over same distance, hence faster **conduction**.

Temperature gradient $= \dfrac{t_2 - t_1}{x}$

where t_1, t_2 = temperatures at points 1 and 2; x = distance

Rate of transfer of heat energy per unit area $= k\dfrac{t_2 - t_1}{x}$

where k = **conductivity** of metal

Wooden handle - low **conductivity** (bad **conductor**).

Metal poker – high conductivity (good conductor)

$\longleftarrow x \longrightarrow$

1   2

Flow of heat energy

- **Conductivity** or **thermal conductivity**. A measure of how good a **conductor** a material is (see also page 114). The rate of heat energy transfer through an object depends on the conductivity of the material and the **temperature gradient**. This is the temperature change with distance along the material. The higher the conductivity and the steeper the gradient, the faster the energy transfer.

- **Convection**. A way in which heat energy is transferred in liquids and gases. If a liquid or gas is heated, it expands, becomes less dense and rises. Cooler, denser liquid or gas then sinks to take its place. Thus a **convection current** is set up.

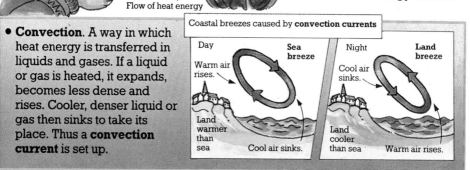

Coastal breezes caused by **convection currents**

Day — Sea breeze. Warm air rises. Land warmer than sea. Cool air sinks.

Night — Land breeze. Cool air sinks. Land cooler than sea. Warm air rises.

* Electrons, 83; Internal energy, Kinetic energy, 9.

- **Radiation**. A way in which heat energy is transferred from a hotter to a cooler place without the **medium*** taking any part in the process. This can occur through a vacuum, unlike **conduction** and **convection**. The term radiation is also often used to refer to the heat energy itself, otherwise known as **radiant heat energy**. This takes the form of **electromagnetic waves***, mainly **infra-red radiation***. When these waves fall on an object, some of their energy is absorbed, increasing the

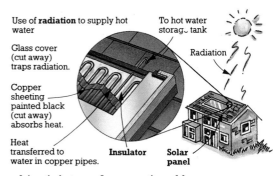

Use of **radiation** to supply hot water

Glass cover (cut away) traps radiation.

Copper sheeting painted black (cut away) absorbs heat.

Heat transferred to water in copper pipes.

To hot water storage tank

Radiation

Insulator   **Solar panel**

object's **internal energy*** and hence its temperature. See also **Leslie's cube**, below.

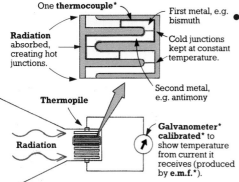

One **thermocouple***

First metal, e.g. bismuth

Radiation absorbed, creating hot junctions.

Cold junctions kept at constant temperature.

Second metal, e.g. antimony

Thermopile

Radiation

Galvanometer* **calibrated*** to show temperature from current it receives (produced by **e.m.f.***).

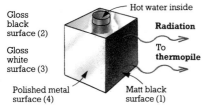

Leslie's cube used to compare powers of **radiation** – numbers show best (1) to worst (4) surface.

Gloss black surface (2)

Gloss white surface (3)

Polished metal surface (4)

Hot water inside

Radiation

To **thermopile**

Matt black surface (1)

- **Thermopile**. A device for measuring **radiation** levels. It consists of two or more **thermocouples*** (normally over 50) joined end to end. Radiation falls on the metal junctions on one side and the temperature difference between these hot junctions and the cold ones on the other side produces an **e.m.f.*** across the thermopile, the size of which indicates how much radiation has been absorbed.

- **Leslie's cube**. A thin-walled, hollow cube (good **conductor**) with different outside surfaces. It is used to show that surfaces vary in their ability to **radiate** and absorb heat energy. Their powers of doing so are compared with an ideal called a **black body**, which absorbs all radiation that falls on it, and is also the best radiator.

- **Greenhouse effect**. The warming effect produced when **radiation** is trapped in a closed area, e.g. a greenhouse. The objects inside absorb the sun's radiation and re-emit lower energy radiation which cannot pass back through the glass. Carbon dioxide in the atmosphere forms a similar barrier, and its level is increasing, hence the air is slowly getting warmer.

- **Vacuum flask**. A flask which keeps its contents at constant temperature. It consists of two glass containers, one inside the other, with a vacuum between them (stopping heat energy transfer by **conduction** and **convection**) and shiny surfaces (minimising transfer by **radiation**).

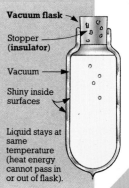

Vacuum flask

Stopper **(insulator)**

Vacuum

Shiny inside surfaces

Liquid stays at same temperature (heat energy cannot pass in or out of flask).

Effects of heat transfer

When an object absorbs or loses **heat energy** (see pages 28-29), its **internal energy*** increases or decreases. This results in either a rise or fall in temperature (the amount of which depends on the **heat capacity** of the object) or a **change of state**.

- **Heat capacity (C)**. The heat energy taken in or given out by an object when its temperature changes by 1 K. It is a property of the object and depends on its mass and the material(s) of which it is made (as well as the temperature and pressure), hence its value is different for every object.

$$Q = C(t_2 - t_1)$$

where Q = heat energy lost or gained; C = **heat capacity**; t_1 and t_2 = temperatures.

The **SI unit*** of **heat capacity** is the joule per kelvin ($J K^{-1}$).

- **Specific heat capacity (c)**. The heat energy taken in or given out when 1 kg of a substance changes temperature by 1 K. It is a property of the substance alone, i.e. there is a set value for each substance (though this changes with pressure and temperature). See also page 114.

$$Q = mc(t_2 - t_1)$$

where m = mass; c = **specific heat capacity**; Q, t_1, t_2 as above.

The **SI unit*** of **specific heat capacity** is the joule per kilogram per kelvin ($J kg^{-1} K^{-1}$).

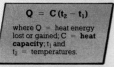

Mass (m) of 2 kg brass (**specific heat capacity** 380 J $kg^{-1} K^{-1}$) heated for a set time. Temperature rises from 303 K (t_1) to 307 K (t_2).

Q (heat gained) = 2 x 380 x (307-303) J

So Q = 3040 J

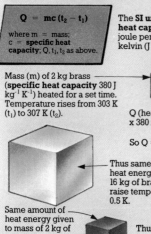

Thus same amount of heat energy taken in by 16 kg of brass would raise temperature by 0.5 K.

Same amount of heat energy given to mass of 2 kg of copper causes temperature rise of 3.8 K.

Thus specific heat capacity of copper is 400 J $kg^{-1} K^{-1}$.

Changes of state

A **change of state** is a change from one **physical state** (the solid, liquid or gaseous state) to another (for more about **physical states**, see page 4). While a change of state is happening, there is no change in temperature. Instead, all the heat energy taken in or given out is used to make or break molecular bonds. This is called **latent heat (L)** – see graphs, page 31. The **specific latent heat (l)** of a substance is a set value, i.e. the heat energy taken in or given out when 1 kg of a substance changes state.

- **Vaporization**. The change of state from liquid to gaseous at a temperature called the **boiling point** of the liquid (it is said to be **boiling**). The term is also used more generally for any change resulting in a gas or vapour, i.e. including also **evaporation** and **sublimation**.

- **Freezing**. The change of state from liquid to solid at the **freezing point** (the same temperature as the **melting point** of the solid).

- **Melting**. The change of state from solid to liquid at a temperature called the **melting point** of the solid.

- **Condensation**. The change of state from gas or vapour to liquid.

- **Evaporation.** The conversion of a liquid to a vapour by the escape of molecules from its surface. It takes place at all temperatures, the rate increasing with any one or a combination of the following: increase in temperature, increase in surface area or decrease in pressure. It is also increased if the vapour is immediately removed from above the liquid by a flow of air. The **latent heat** (see changes of state) needed for evaporation is taken from the liquid itself which cools and in turn cools its surroundings.

- **Sublimation.** The conversion of a substance from a solid directly to a gas, or vice-versa, without passing through the liquid state.

Dry ice (solid carbon dioxide) **sublimes**.

Changes of state. Temperature remains constant (see graph below).

Changes due to cooling. Heat energy which would have been lost (lowering temperature) used instead (as **latent heat**) to make bonds between molecules.

Changes due to heating. Heat energy taken in, which would have raised the temperature, used instead (as **latent heat**) to break bonds.

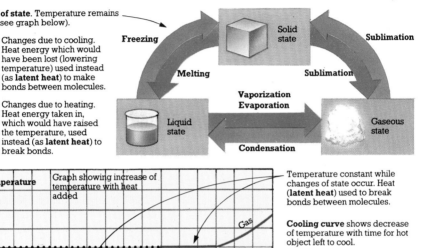

Solid state
Freezing **Sublimation**
Melting Sublimation
Vaporization **Evaporation**
Liquid state Gaseous state
Condensation

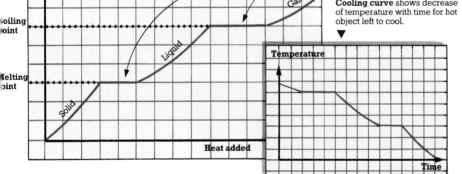

Temperature

Graph showing increase of temperature with heat added

Gas

Boiling point

Liquid

Melting point

Solid

Heat added

Temperature constant while changes of state occur. Heat (**latent heat**) used to break bonds between molecules.

Cooling curve shows decrease of temperature with time for hot object left to cool.

Temperature

Time

- **Specific latent heat of vaporization.** The heat energy taken in when 1 kg of a substance changes from a liquid to a gas at its **boiling point**. It is the same as the heat given out when the process is reversed.

- **Specific latent heat of fusion.** The heat energy taken in when 1 kg of a substance changes from a solid to a liquid at its **melting point**. It is the same as the heat given out when the process is reversed. See also page 114.

$$Q = ml$$
where Q = heat energy lost or gained by object; m = mass, l = **specific latent heat**.

The **SI unit*** of **specific latent heat** is the joule per kilogram (J kg^{-1}).

Expansion on heating

Most substances expand when heated – their molecules move faster and further apart. The extent of this expansion (**expansivity**) depends on **intermolecular forces***. For the same amount of heat applied (at constant pressure), solids expand least, as their molecules are closest together and so have the strongest forces between them. Liquids expand more, and gases the most.

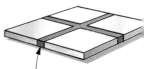

Expansion of solids on heating must be taken into account in building work.

Rubberized compound put between paving stones

- **Bimetallic strip.** A device which shows the expansion of solids on heating. It is made up of two different strips of metal, joined along their (equal) length. When heated or cooled, both metals expand or contract (respectively), but at different rates, so the strip bends. Such strips are used in **thermostats**.

Thermostat (temperature regulator)

Strip bends outwards as it heats up. Circuit is broken at point determined by knob. As surroundings cool it bends back, and heater is switched back on.

Bimetallic strip (invar and brass)

Electrical contacts

Metal bar

Insulating block

Knob controls temperature at which heater switches off or back on by setting position of metal bar and its contact.

To heater

- **Linear expansivity (α).** A measurement of the fraction of its original length by which a solid expands for a temperature rise of 1K.

- **Superficial** or **areal expansivity (β).** A measurement of the fraction of its original area by which a solid expands for a temperature rise of 1K.

For solids or liquids:

Note the only relevant measurement for liquids is **cubic expansivity**. It is either **real** or **apparent** (see page 33), hence so is change in volume in formula.

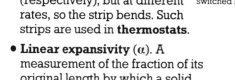

$$\text{Expansivity (linear, superficial or cubic)} = \frac{\text{change in (length, area or volume)}}{\text{original (length, area or volume)} \times \text{temperature rise}}$$

For gases:

$$\text{Cubic expansivity} = \frac{\text{change in volume at constant pressure}}{\text{volume at } 0°C \ (273K) \times \text{temperature rise}}$$

- **Cubic** or **volume expansivity** (γ). A measurement of the fraction of its original volume by which a substance expands for a temperature rise of 1K. It is the same for all gases (at constant pressure) when they are assumed to behave as **ideal gases**. Since gases expand by very large amounts, the original volume is always taken at 0°C so that proper comparisons can be made (this is not felt to be necessary with solids or liquids as the changes are so small).

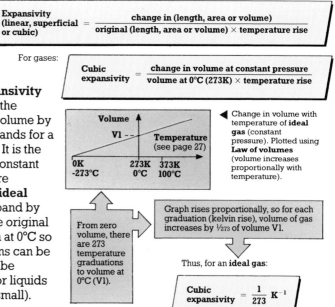

Volume

V1

Temperature (see page 27)

| 0K | 273K | 373K |
| -273°C | 0°C | 100°C |

Change in volume with temperature of **ideal gas** (constant pressure). Plotted using **Law of volumes** (volume increases proportionally with temperature).

From zero volume, there are 273 temperature graduations to volume at 0°C (V1).

Graph rises proportionally, so for each graduation (kelvin rise), volume of gas increases by $\frac{1}{273}$ of volume V1.

Thus, for an **ideal gas**:

$$\text{Cubic expansivity} = \frac{1}{273} \ K^{-1}$$

* Intermolecular forces, 7.

- **Real** or **absolute cubic expansivity**. An accurate measurement of the fraction of its volume by which a liquid expands for a temperature rise of 1K.

- **Apparent cubic expansivity**. A measurement of the fraction of its volume by which a liquid apparently expands for a temperature rise of 1K.

In fact, the heat applied also causes very slight expansion of the container, so its calibrated measurements are no longer valid.

- **Anomalous expansion**. The phenomenon whereby some liquids contract instead of expanding when the temperature rises within a certain range (e.g. water between 0°C and 4°C).

Behaviour of gases

All gases behave in a similar way, and there are several **gas laws** which describe their behaviour (see below). An **ideal gas** is a theoretical gas which, by definition, exactly obeys **Boyle's law** at all temperatures and pressures, but in fact also obeys the two other laws as well. When real gases are at normal temperatures and pressures, they show approximately ideal behaviour (the higher the temperature and the lower the pressure, the better the approximation), hence the laws may be generally applied.

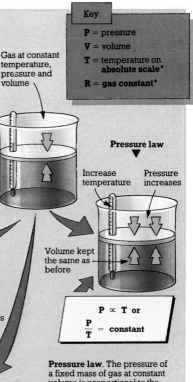

Gas at constant temperature, pressure and volume

Pressure law ▼

Increase temperature — Pressure increases

Volume kept the same as before

$$P \propto T \text{ or}$$
$$\frac{P}{T} = \text{constant}$$

Pressure law. The pressure of a fixed mass of gas at constant volume is proportional to the temperature on the **absolute scale***. For example, if the temperature increases but the volume is kept the same, the pressure inside the gas increases proportionally – the molecules move faster, so hit the container walls more often. Note the pressure exerted on the gas to keep the volume constant must increase by the same amount as that exerted by it.

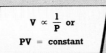

$$V \propto \frac{1}{P} \text{ or}$$
$$PV = \text{constant}$$

Boyle's law ▼

Increase pressure

Volume decreases

Temperature kept the same as before

Boyle's law. The volume of a fixed mass of gas at constant temperature is inversely proportional to the pressure. For example, if the pressure on the gas increases, the volume decreases proportionally – the molecules move closer together. Note the pressure exerted by the gas increases by the same amount as that exerted on it (the molecules hit the container walls more often).

Law of volumes. The volume of a fixed mass of gas at constant pressure is proportional to the temperature on the **absolute scale***. For example, if the temperature increases and the pressure is kept the same, the volume increases proportionally (given an expandable container) – the molecules move faster and further apart. Note the pressure exerted by the gas remains constant, like that exerted on it (the molecules hit the walls at the same frequency – they have more space, but greater energy).

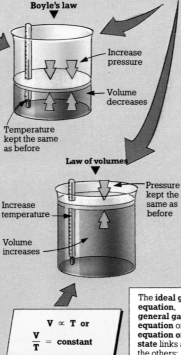

Law of volumes ▼

Increase temperature

Volume increases

Pressure kept the same as before

$$V \propto T \text{ or}$$
$$\frac{V}{T} = \text{constant}$$

The **ideal gas equation**, **general gas equation** or **equation of state** links all the others:

For one **mole*** of gas:

$$\frac{PV}{T} = R \text{ or } PV = RT$$

Waves

Mechanical wave (**transverse wave**) passes along string.

Each particle **oscillates** and returns to rest.

All **waves** transport energy without permanently displacing the **medium*** through which they travel. They are also called **progressive** or **travelling waves**, as the energy travels from a source to surrounding points (but see also **stationary wave**, page 43). There are two main types – **mechanical waves**, such as sound waves, and **electromagnetic waves** (see page 44). In all cases, the **wave motion** is regular and repetitive (i.e. **periodic motion** – see page 16) in the form of **oscillations** – regular

▼ Displacement/time graph for **oscillation** of one particle

Displacement (direction and distance from mean position)

Amplitude is maximum displacement. The greater it is, the more energy wave carries.

Mean position (position when at rest)

Time

Time taken by one oscillation is a **period** (see also page 16).

changes between two extremes. In mechanical waves it is particles (molecules) that oscillate and in electromagnetic waves it is electric and magnetic fields.

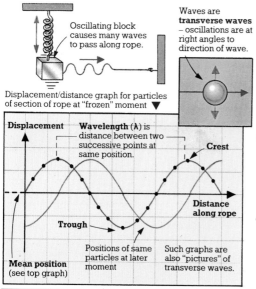

Oscillating block causes many waves to pass along rope.

Waves are **transverse waves** – oscillations are at right angles to direction of wave.

Displacement/distance graph for particles of section of rope at "frozen" moment ▼

Displacement

Wavelength (λ) is distance between two successive points at same position.

Crest

Distance along rope

Trough

Positions of same particles at later moment

Such graphs are also "pictures" of transverse waves.

Mean position (see top graph)

- **Transverse waves**. Waves in which the oscillations are at right angles to the direction of energy (wave) movement, e.g. water waves (oscillation of particles) and all **electromagnetic waves*** (oscillation of fields – see introduction).

- **Crests** or **peaks**. Points where a wave causes maximum positive displacement of the **medium***. The crests of some waves, e.g. water waves, can be seen as they travel.

- **Troughs**. Points where a wave causes maximum negative displacement of the **medium***. The troughs of some waves, e.g. water waves, can be seen as they travel.

- **Wavefront**. Any line or section taken through an advancing wave which joins all points which are in the same position in their oscillations. Wavefronts are usually at right angles to the direction of the waves and can have any shape, e.g. **circular** and **straight wavefronts**.

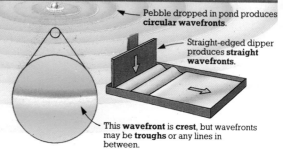

Pebble dropped in pond produces **circular wavefronts**.

Straight-edged dipper produces **straight wavefronts**.

This **wavefront** is crest, but wavefronts may be **troughs** or any lines in between.

* Electromagnetic waves, 44; Medium, 115.

- **Longitudinal waves.** Waves in which the oscillations are along the line of the direction of wave movement, e.g. sound waves. They are all **mechanical waves** (see introduction), i.e. it is particles which oscillate.

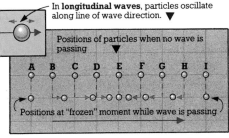

In **longitudinal waves**, particles oscillate along line of wave direction. ▼

Positions of particles when no wave is passing ▼

A B C D E F G H I

Positions at "frozen" moment while wave is passing

Graph of particles above at "frozen" moment. Graph not in this case "picture" of wave (see second graph, page 34). ▼

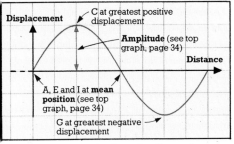

Displacement

C at greatest positive displacement

Amplitude (see top graph, page 34)

Distance

A, E and I at **mean position** (see top graph, page 34)

G at greatest negative displacement

Graph of pressure or density against distance for **longitudinal wave** shows **compressions** and **rarefactions**. ▼

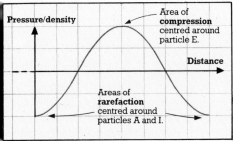

Pressure/density

Area of **compression** centred around particle E.

Distance

Areas of **rarefaction** centred around particles A and I.

- **Compressions.** Regions along a **longitudinal wave** where the pressure and density of the molecules is higher than when no wave is passing.

- **Rarefactions.** Regions along a **longitudinal wave** where the pressure and density of the molecules is lower than when no wave is passing.

- **Wave speed.** The distance moved by a wave in one second. It depends on the **medium*** through which the wave is travelling.

$$\text{Wave speed} = \frac{\text{distance moved by wave}}{\text{time}}$$

$$= \frac{\text{number of waves passing point} \times \textbf{wavelength}}{\text{time}}$$

$$= \frac{\textbf{frequency} \times}{\textbf{wavelength}}$$

Hence:

$$s = f\lambda$$
where s = **wave speed**; f = **frequency**; λ = **wavelength**.

- **Frequency (f).** The number of oscillations which occur in one second when waves pass a given point (see also page 16). It is equal to the number of **wavelengths** (see second graph, page 34) per second.

- **Attenuation.** The gradual decrease in **amplitude** (see top graph, page 34) of a wave as it passes through matter and loses energy. The amplitudes of oscillations occurring further from the source are less than those of oscillations nearer to it. This can be seen as an overall **damping***, although this term actually refers to the gradual decrease in amplitude of the oscillations of any single particle.

Graph showing **attenuated** wave

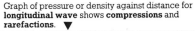

Displacement

Amplitude decreases

Distance from source

- **Wave intensity.** A measurement of the energy carried by a wave. It is worked out as the amount of energy falling on unit area per second. It depends both on the **frequency** and **amplitude** of the wave.

Reflection, refraction and diffraction

An obstacle or a change of environment causes a wave to undergo **reflection**, **refraction** or **diffraction**. These are different types of change in wave direction and often also result in changes in the shape of the **wavefronts***. For more about the reflection and refraction of light waves, see pages 46-53.

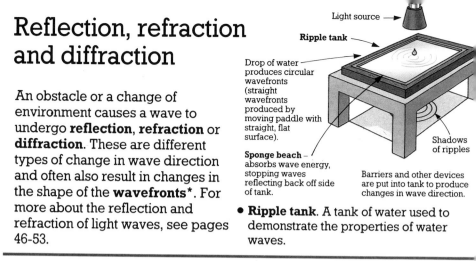

Light source →

Ripple tank ─

Drop of water produces circular wavefronts (straight wavefronts produced by moving paddle with straight, flat surface).

Sponge beach – absorbs wave energy, stopping waves reflecting back off side of tank.

Shadows of ripples

Barriers and other devices are put into tank to produce changes in wave direction.

- **Ripple tank.** A tank of water used to demonstrate the properties of water waves.

- **Reflection.** The change in direction of a wave due to its bouncing off a boundary between two **media***. A wave that has undergone reflection is called a **reflected wave**. The shape of its wavefronts depends on the shape of the **incident wavefronts** and the shape of the boundary. For more about the reflection of light waves, see pages 46-49.

Examples of **reflected wave** shapes

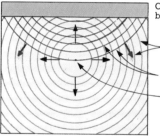

Circular wavefronts hitting straight boundary produce circular wavefronts.

Circular wavefronts (**incident waves**)

Circular wavefronts (**reflected waves**)

Source, e.g. drop of water

Circular wavefronts hitting concave boundary producing straight wavefronts in this case (i.e. with ship at this distance).

Ship's hooter produces sound waves.

Circular wavefronts (**incident waves**)

Straight wavefronts (**reflected waves**)

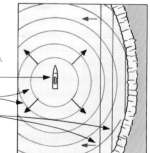

Straight wavefronts hitting straight boundary produce straight wavefronts.

Rear view car mirror

Light waves from car headlights behind

Straight wavefronts (**incident waves**)

Straight wavefronts (**reflected waves**)

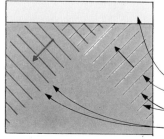

- **Incident wave.** A wave that is travelling towards a boundary between two **media***. Its wavefronts are called **incident wavefronts**.

- **Diffraction.** The bending effect which occurs when a wave meets an obstacle or passes through an aperture. The amount the wave bends depends on the size of the obstacle or aperture compared to the **wavelength*** of the wave. The smaller the obstacle or aperture by comparison, the more the wave bends.

* Medium, 115; Wavefront, Wavelength, 34.

- **Refraction**. The change in direction of a wave when it moves into a new **medium**⋆ which causes it to travel at a different speed. A wave which has undergone refraction is called a **refracted wave**. Its **wavelength**⋆ increases or decreases with the change in speed, but there is no change in the **frequency**⋆. For more about the refraction of light waves, see pages 50-53.

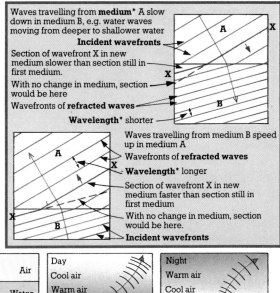

Waves travelling from **medium**⋆ A slow down in medium B, e.g. water waves moving from deeper to shallower water

Incident wavefronts

Section of wavefront X in new medium slower than section still in first medium.

With no change in medium, section would be here

Wavefronts of **refracted waves**

Wavelength⋆ shorter

Waves travelling from medium B speed up in medium A

Wavefronts of **refracted waves**

Wavelength⋆ longer

Section of wavefront X in new medium faster than section still in first medium.

With no change in medium, section would be here.

Incident wavefronts

Other examples:

| Air |
| Water |

Waves slow down on entering a denser medium.

| Air |
| Water |

They speed up on entering a less dense medium.

| Day |
| Cool air |
| Warm air |

So waves slow down on entering a cooler medium ▶

| Night |
| Warm air |
| Cool air |

(cooler means denser). They speed up on entering a warmer medium.

- **Refractive index (n)**. A number which indicates the power of refraction of a given **medium**⋆ relative to a previous medium. It is found by dividing the speed of the **incident wave** in the first medium by the speed of the **refracted wave** in the given medium (subscript numbers are used – see formula). The **absolute refractive index** of a medium is the speed of light in that medium compared to the speed of light in a vacuum (or, generally, in air). For more about refractive index and light, see page 50.

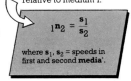

This means **refractive index** of **medium**⋆ 2 relative to medium 1.

$$_1n_2 = \frac{s_1}{s_2}$$

where s_1, s_2 = speeds in first and second **media**⋆.

Diffraction of waves (sound waves) round obstacle

Obstacle small compared to **wavelength**⋆ (wavelength of sound is about 2 m) – a lot of diffraction, so no "shadow" formed.

Obstacle about same size as wavelength – some diffraction, so small "shadow" formed, i.e. area through which no waves pass

Obstacle large compared to wavelength – almost no diffraction, so large "shadow" formed.

Diffraction of water waves passing through aperture (slit).

Aperture wide compared to **wavelength**⋆ – little diffraction.

Aperture about same size as wavelength – some diffraction.

Aperture narrow compared to wavelength – a lot of diffraction.

Wave interference

When two or more waves travel in the same or different directions in a given space, variations in the size of the resulting disturbance occur at points where they meet (see **principle of superposition**, page 39). This effect is called **interference**. When interference is demonstrated, e.g. in a **ripple tank***, sources which produce **coherent waves** are always used, i.e. waves with the same wavelength and frequency, and either **in phase** or with a constant **phase difference** (see **phase**). This ensures that the interference produces a regular, identifiable **interference pattern** of disturbance (see picture, page 39). The use of non-coherent waves would result only in a constantly-changing confusion of waves.

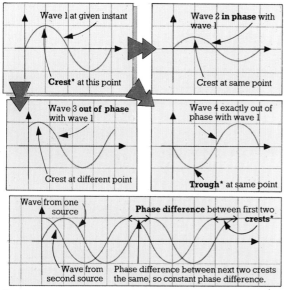

Wave 1 at given instant

Wave 2 **in phase** with wave 1

Crest* at this point

Crest at same point

Wave 3 **out of phase** with wave 1

Wave 4 exactly out of phase with wave 1

Crest at different point

Trough* at same point

Wave from one source

Phase difference between first two **crests***

Wave from second source

Phase difference between next two crests the same, so constant phase difference.

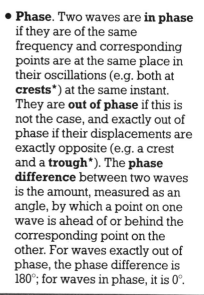

- **Phase**. Two waves are **in phase** if they are of the same frequency and corresponding points are at the same place in their oscillations (e.g. both at **crests***) at the same instant. They are **out of phase** if this is not the case, and exactly out of phase if their displacements are exactly opposite (e.g. a crest and a **trough***). The **phase difference** between two waves is the amount, measured as an angle, by which a point on one wave is ahead of or behind the corresponding point on the other. For waves exactly out of phase, the phase difference is 180°; for waves in phase, it is 0°.

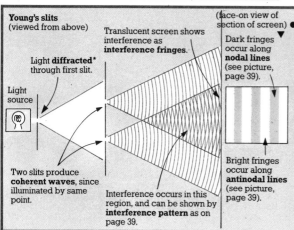

Young's slits (viewed from above)

Translucent screen shows interference as **interference fringes**.

Light **diffracted*** through first slit.

Light source

Two slits produce **coherent waves**, since illuminated by same point.

Interference occurs in this region, and can be shown by **interference pattern** as on page 39.

(face-on view of section of screen)

Dark fringes occur along **nodal lines** (see picture, page 39).

Bright fringes occur along **antinodal lines** (see picture, page 39).

- **Young's slits**. An arrangement of narrow, parallel slits, used to create two sources of **coherent** light (see introduction). They are needed because coherent light waves cannot be produced (for studying interference) as easily as other coherent waves, as light wave emission is usually random. The interference of the light **diffracted*** through the slits is seen on a screen as light and dark bands called **interference fringes**.

* Crests, 34; **Diffraction, Ripple tank,** 36; **Troughs,** 34.

- **Principle of superposition**. States that, when the **superposition** of two or more waves occurs at a point (i.e. two or more waves come together), the resultant displacement is equal to the sum of the displacements (positive or negative) of the individual waves.

- **Constructive interference**. The increase in disturbance (reinforcement) which results from the **superposition** of two waves which are **in phase** (see **phase**).

- **Destructive interference**. The decrease in disturbance which results from the **superposition** of two waves which are exactly **out of phase**.

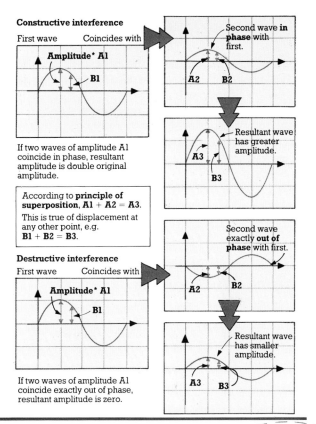

Constructive interference

First wave   Coincides with

Amplitude* A1
B1

Second wave **in phase** with first.
A2   B2

Resultant wave has greater amplitude.
A3
B3

If two waves of amplitude A1 coincide in phase, resultant amplitude is double original amplitude.

According to **principle of superposition**, $A1 + A2 = A3$. This is true of displacement at any other point, e.g. $B1 + B2 = B3$.

Destructive interference

First wave   Coincides with

Amplitude* A1
B1

Second wave exactly **out of phase** with first.
A2   B2

Resultant wave has smaller amplitude.
A3   B3

If two waves of amplitude A1 coincide exactly out of phase, resultant amplitude is zero.

- **Nodes** or **nodal points**. Points at which **destructive interference** is continually occurring, and which are consequently regularly points of minimum disturbance, i.e. points where **crest*** meets **trough*** or **compression*** meets **rarefaction*** A **nodal line** is a line consisting entirely of nodes.

- **Antinodes** or **antinodal points**. Points at which **constructive interference** is continually occurring, and which are consequently regularly points of maximum disturbance, i.e. points where two **crests***, **troughs***, **compressions*** or **rarefactions*** meet. An **antinodal line** is a line consisting entirely of antinodes.

Interference pattern at "frozen" moment (not all antinodal/nodal lines shown).

Two sources (**S1** and **S2**) produce **coherent waves**, in this case **in phase**.

Crest* or **compression***

Trough* or **rarefaction***

Antinodal line (**constructive interference**)

Nodal line (**destructive interference**). If waves are same amplitude, disturbance at all points along it is zero.

Depending on waves, antinodal lines indicate areas of rough water, loud sound or bright light (see also **Young's slits** picture, page 38).

Nodal lines indicate calm water, soft sound or darkness (see also **Young's slits** picture).

S1

S2

* **Amplitude**, 34; **Compressions**, 35; **Crests**, 34; **Rarefactions**, 35; **Troughs**, 34.

Sound waves

Sound waves, also called **acoustic waves**, are **longitudinal waves*** – waves which consist of particles oscillating along the same line as the waves travel, creating areas of high and low pressure (**compressions*** and **rarefactions***). They can travel through solids, liquids and gases and have a wide range of **frequencies***. Those with frequencies between about 20 and 20,000 **Hertz*** (the **sonic range**) can be detected by the human ear and are what is commonly referred to as sound (for more about perception of sound, see pages 42-43). Others, with higher and lower frequencies, are known as **ultrasound** and **infrasound**. The study of the behaviour of sound waves is called **acoustics**.

- **Ultrasound.** Sound composed of **ultrasonic waves** – waves with **frequencies*** above the range of the human ear, i.e. above 20,000 **Hertz***. They have a number of uses.

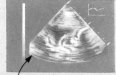
Scan of baby in mother's womb

Ultrasound is used in **ultrasound scanning** of the human body (uses **echoes** – see page 41).

Bone, fat and muscle all reflect **ultrasonic waves** differently. Reflected waves (**echoes**) converted into electrical pulses which form an image (scan) on a screen.

- **Infrasound.** Sound composed of **infrasonic waves** – waves with **frequencies*** below the range of the human ear, i.e. below 20 **Hertz***. At present they have few technical uses, as they can be distressing to humans.

Behaviour of sound waves

- **Speed of sound.** The speed at which sound waves move. It depends on the type and temperature of the **medium*** through which they travel. The speed of sound waves travelling through dry air at 0°C is 331 m s^{-1}, but this increases if the air temperature increases.

- **Subsonic speed.** A speed below the **speed of sound** in the same **medium*** and under the same conditions.

- **Supersonic speed.** A speed above the **speed of sound** in the same **medium*** and under the same conditions.

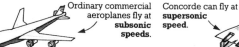
Ordinary commercial aeroplanes fly at **subsonic speeds**.
Concorde can fly at **supersonic speed**.

- **Sonic boom.** A loud bang heard when a **shock wave** (see below right) produced by an aeroplane moving at **supersonic speed** passes a listener.

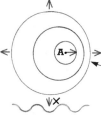

As aeroplane (A) travels forward, it creates **longitudinal waves*** in air, i.e. areas of high and low pressure (**compressions*** and **rarefactions***).

Wavefronts* can "get away" from aeroplane and begin to disperse.

Listener at X will hear waves as sound (a "whoosh" of air – as well as separate sound of engines).

Supersonic aeroplane (A) overtakes its wavefronts while creating more, so they overlap.

Causes large build up of pressure (**shock wave**) pushed in front of aeroplane and unable to "get away", like bow wave of ship (if ship travelling faster than water waves it creates).

Listener at X will hear wave as sudden loud **sonic boom**.

* **Compressions, Frequency,** 35; **Hertz,** 16 (**Frequency**); **Longitudinal waves,** 35; **Medium,** 115; **Rarefactions,** 35; **Wavefront,** 34.

Echo. A sound wave which has been reflected off a surface, and is heard after the original sound. Echoes, normally those of **ultrasonic waves**, are often used to locate objects and determine their exact position (by measuring the time the echo takes to return to the source). This technique has a number of names, each normally used in a slightly different context, though the distinctions between them are unclear.

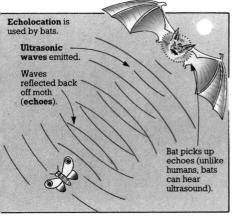

Sonar (derived from **s**ound **na**vigation and **r**anging)

Ultrasonic waves emitted by device below ship.

Waves reflected back by submarine (**echoes**).

Echoes picked up by sensing equipment below ship. Converted to electrical pulses which form an image of submarine on a screen in the ship.

Ultrasound scanning (see page 40) is one example. Others are **echo-sounding** and **sonar**, both of which have marine connotations (echo-sounding normally refers to using echoes to measure the depth of water below a ship, sonar to using them to detect objects under water).

Echolocation usually describes the way animals use echoes to find prey or avoid obstacles in the dark.

Echolocation is used by bats.

Ultrasonic waves emitted.

Waves reflected back off moth (**echoes**).

Bat picks up echoes (unlike humans, bats can hear ultrasound).

- **Reverberation**. The effect whereby a sound appears to persist for longer than it actually took to produce. It occurs when the time taken for the **echo** to return to the source is so short that the original and reflected wave cannot be distinguished. If the wave is reflected off many surfaces, then the sound is enhanced further.

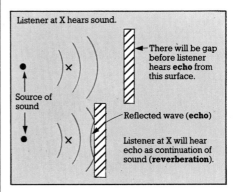

Listener at X hears sound.

There will be gap before listener hears **echo** from this surface.

Source of sound

Reflected wave (**echo**)

Listener at X will hear echo as continuation of sound (**reverberation**).

- **Doppler effect**. The change in **frequency*** of the sound heard when either the listener or the source moves relative to the other. If the distance between them is decreasing, a higher frequency sound is heard than that actually produced. If it is increasing, a lower frequency sound is heard.

Doppler effect

Train hoots while approaching and passing listener at X.

Wavefronts* move out at **speed of sound**.

Wavefronts closer together here because train moving forward while producing sound waves. Heard at X as sound of higher **frequency***.

Lower frequency sound will be heard when train has passed.

* **Frequency**, 35; **Wavefront**, 34.

Perception of sound

Sounds heard by the ear can be pleasant or unpleasant. When the waveform of a **sound wave** (see pages 40-41) repeats itself regularly, the sound is usually judged to be pleasant. However, when it is unrepeated and irregular, the sound is thought of as a **noise**. Every sound has a particular **loudness** and **pitch** and many, especially musical sounds, are produced by **stationary waves**.

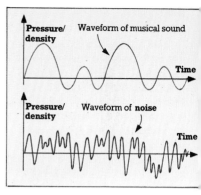

- **Loudness**. The size of the sensation produced when sound waves fall on the ear. It is subjective, depending on the sensitivity of the ear, but is directly related to the **wave intensity*** of the waves. It is most often measured in **decibels** (**dB**), but also, more accurately, in **phons** (these take into account the fact that the ear is not equally sensitive to sounds of all **frequencies***).

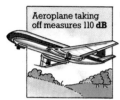

Aeroplane taking off measures 110 **dB**

- **Pitch**. The perceived **frequency*** of a sound wave, i.e. the frequency heard as sound. A high pitched sound has a high frequency and a low pitched sound a low frequency.

- **Beats**. The regular variation in **loudness** with time which is heard when two sounds of slightly different **frequency*** are heard together. It is a result of **interference*** between the two waves. The **beat frequency** is equal to the difference in frequency between the two sounds (see picture). The closer together the frequency of the sounds, the slower the beats.

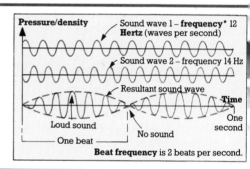

Beat frequency is 2 beats per second.

Musical sounds

All music is based on some kind of **musical scale**. This is a series of **notes** (sounds of specific **pitch**), arranged from low to high pitch with certain **intervals** between them (a musical interval is a spacing in **frequency***, rather than time). The notes are arranged so that the maximum number of pleasant sounds can be obtained. What is regarded as a pleasant sound depends on culture – Eastern music is based on a different scale to Western music.

Western **musical scale** is based on **diatonic scale** – consists of 8 **notes** (white notes on piano) ranging from lower to upper C.

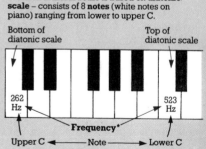

Black notes have **frequencies*** between those of notes on **diatonic scale**. Together with these, they form **chromatic scale**.

* **Frequency**, 35; **Interference**, 38; **Wave intensity**, 35.

- **Stationary** or **standing wave**. A wave that does not appear to move. It is not in fact a true wave, but is instead made up of two waves of the same velocity and **frequency*** continuously moving in opposite directions between two fixed points (most commonly the ends of a plucked string or wire). The repeated crossing of the waves results in **interference*** – when the waves are **in phase***, the resultant **amplitude*** is large, and when they are **out of phase***, it is small or zero. At certain points (the **nodes**), it is always zero. The amplitude and frequency of a stationary wave in a string or wire determines those of the sound waves it produces in the air – the length and tension of the string or wire determines the range of frequencies, and hence the pitch of the sound produced.

Formation of stationary wave

Waves A and B (same **amplitude***) moving in opposite directions between two fixed points.

Resultant wave at time t = 0. Amplitude doubled.

Resultant wave at time t = 1. Amplitude zero.

At time t = 2, resultant wave has same amplitude as at t = 0, but is transposed, i.e. **crests*** where there were **troughs*** and vice versa.

Nodes

Antinodes (see below)

Resultant wave continuously moving rapidly between position held at t = 0 and that held at t = 2. Wave observed appears stationary.

Sonometer. Piece of apparatus used to demonstrate **stationary waves**. When plucked, wire vibrates and sound box amplifies sound caused by vibration.

Hollow box

Stationary wave

Fixed bridge

Positions of zero vibration (**nodes**)

Positions of maximum vibration (**antinodes**).

Fixed bridge

Movable bridge. Can be adjusted to change length of wire and so alter **pitch** of note.

Weights. Can be adjusted to change tension of wire and so alter pitch of note.

- **Modes of vibration**. The same note played on different instruments, although recognizable as the same note, has a quite distinct sound quality (**timbre**), characteristic to the instrument. This is because, although the main, strongest vibration is the same for each note whatever the instrument (its **frequency*** is the **fundamental frequency**), vibrations at other frequencies (**overtones**) are also produced at the same time. The set of vibrations specific to an instrument are its modes of vibration.

Lowest **mode of vibration** (**fundamental frequency**) of note on given instrument.

If frequencies of **overtones** are simple multiples of fundamental frequency, also called **harmonics**.

1st overtone (2nd harmonic, i.e. frequency doubled. Note fundamental is 1st harmonic)

2nd overtone (note this is 4th harmonic, i.e. in this case there is no 3rd harmonic)

Combined modes of vibration (i.e. all three put together). Characteristic waveform of note for this instrument.

Same note played on different instrument may look like this.

* **Amplitude, Crests**, 34; **Frequency**, 35; **In phase**, 38 (**Phase**), **Interference**, 38; **Out of phase**, 38 (**Phase**); **Troughs**, 34.

Electromagnetic waves

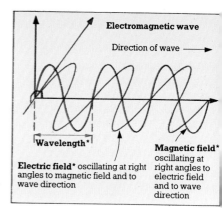

Electromagnetic wave

Direction of wave ⟶

Electromagnetic waves are **transverse waves***, consisting of oscillating **electric** and **magnetic fields***. They have a wide range of **frequencies***, can travel through all **media***, including vacuums, and, when absorbed, cause a rise in temperature (see **infra-red radiation**). **Radio waves** and some **X-rays** are emitted when free

Wavelength*

Electric field* oscillating at right angles to magnetic field and to wave direction

Magnetic field* oscillating at right angles to electric field and to wave direction

electrons* are accelerated or decelerated, e.g. as a result of a collision. All other types occur when molecules change energy states (see page 84). All except radio waves occur as random pulses called **photons** (see **quantum theory**, page 85), rather than a continuous stream.

Electromagnetic spectrum (range of electromagnetic waves). Five main sections are **wavebands**, i.e. particular ranges of **frequencies*** **and wavelengths*** within which the waves all have the same characteristic properties.

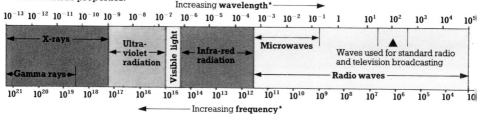

Increasing **wavelength*** ⟶

10^{-13} 10^{-12} 10^{-11} 10^{-10} 10^{-9} 10^{-8} 10^{-7} 10^{-6} 10^{-5} 10^{-4} 10^{-3} 10^{-2} 10^{-1} 1 10^1 10^2 10^3 10^4 10^5

X-rays | Ultra-violet radiation | Visible light | Infra-red radiation | Microwaves | Waves used for standard radio and television broadcasting

Gamma rays | Radio waves

10^{21} 10^{20} 10^{19} 10^{18} 10^{17} 10^{16} 10^{15} 10^{14} 10^{13} 10^{12} 10^{11} 10^{10} 10^9 10^8 10^7 10^6 10^5 10^4 10

⟵ Increasing **frequency***

- **Gamma rays (γ-rays).** Electromagnetic waves emitted by **radioactive*** substances (see also page 86). They are in the same **waveband** and have the same properties as **X-rays**, but are produced in a different way and are at the top end of the band with regard to energy.

X-radiography produces pictures (**radiographs**) of inside the body. **X-rays** pass through tissue but are absorbed by bones, so bones appear opaque.

Human elbow

- **X-rays** or **Röntgen rays.** Electromagnetic waves which **ionize*** gases they pass through, cause **phosphorescence** and bring about chemical changes on photographic plates. They are produced in **X-ray tubes*** and have many applications.

- **Ultra-violet radiation (UV radiation).** Electromagnetic waves produced, for example, when an electric current is passed through **ionized*** gas between two **electrodes***. They are also emitted by the sun, but only small quantities reach the earth's surface (as most are absorbed by atoms in the various layers of the atmosphere). These small quantities are vital to life (playing the key part in **photosynthesis** – the production of glucose by plants), but larger amounts are dangerous. Ultra-violet radiation causes **fluorescence**, e.g. when produced in **fluorescent tubes***, and also a variety of chemical reactions, e.g. tanning of the skin.

* **Electric field**, 58; **Electrode**, 66; **Electrons**, 83; **Fluorescent tube**, 80(Discharge tube); **Frequency**, 35; **Ionization**, 88; **Magnetic field**, 72; **Medium**, 115; **Radioactivity**, 86; **Transverse waves**, **Wavelength**, 34; **X-ray tube**, 81.

- **Phosphorescence.** A phenomenon shown by certain substances (**phosphors**). When they are hit by short **wavelength*** electromagnetic waves, e.g. **gamma rays** or **X-rays**, they absorb these and emit **visible light**, i.e. waves of longer wavelength. This emission may continue after the gamma or X-rays have stopped. If it only occurs briefly afterwards in rapid flashes, these are called **scintillations** (see also **scintillation counter**, page 90).

- **Fluorescence.** A phenomenon shown by certain substances. When they are hit by **ultra-violet radiation**, they absorb this and emit **visible light**, i.e. light waves of a longer **wavelength***. This emission stops as soon as the ultra-violet radiation stops.

- **Infra-red radiation (IR radiation).** The electromagnetic waves most commonly produced by hot objects and therefore those which are most frequently the cause of temperature rises (see introduction and **radiation**, page 29). They can be used to form **thermal images** on special infra-red sensitive film, exposed by heat, rather than light.

Thermal image of lake water used as coolant for **nuclear power station*** (taken from a satellite). .

Warmest water brown, coolest blue. Each colour represents about one degree temperature difference.

- **Visible light.** Electromagnetic waves which the eye can detect. They are produced by the sun, by **discharge tubes*** and by any substance heated until it glows (emission of light due to heating is called **incandescence**). They cause chemical changes, e.g. on photographic film, and the different **wavelengths*** in the **waveband** are seen as different colours (see page 55).

- **Microwaves.** Very short **radio waves** used in **radar** (**ra**dio **d**etection **and r**anging) to determine the position of an object by the time it takes for a reflected wave to return to the source (see also **sonar**, page 41). **Microwave ovens** use microwaves to cook food rapidly.

- **Radio waves.** Electromagnetic waves produced when free **electrons*** in radio aerials are made to oscillate (and are hence accelerated) by an **electric field***. The fact that the frequency of the oscillations is imposed by the field means that the waves occur as a regular stream, rather than randomly. They are used to communicate over distances.

Magnetron connected to normal electricity supply produces **microwaves**.

Microwaves pass through food container, but not metal lining of oven. Cause water, fat or sugar molecules in food to oscillate, increasing **internal energy*** and cooking the food.

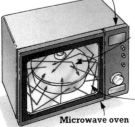

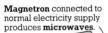
Microwave oven

Waves reflected off oven walls, so cook food evenly.

Radio waves with short **wavelengths*** can penetrate ionosphere, hence are used to communicate over long distances via satellites.

Radio waves with long **wavelengths*** reflected within ionosphere, hence are used to transmit information from place to place on same area of earth's surface.

Ionosphere (region of **ionized*** gas around the earth)

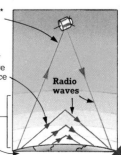

Radio waves

Earth

* **Discharge tube**, 80; **Electric field**, 58; **Electrons**, 83; **Internal energy**, 9; **Ionization**, 88; **Nuclear power station**, 94; **Wavelength**, 34.

45

Light

Light consists of **electromagnetic waves*** of particular **frequencies*** and **wavelengths*** (see pages 44-45), but is commonly referred to and diagrammatically represented as taking the form of **rays**. Such a ray is actually a line (arrow) which indicates the path taken by the light waves, i.e. the direction in which the energy is being carried.

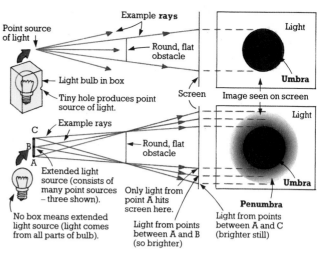

Point source of light

Example **rays**

Round, flat obstacle

Light bulb in box

Tiny hole produces point source of light.

Screen

Image seen on screen

Light

Umbra

Example rays

C
B
A

Round, flat obstacle

Extended light source (consists of many point sources – three shown).

No box means extended light source (light comes from all parts of bulb).

Only light from point A hits screen here.

Light from points between A and B (so brighter)

Light from points between A and C (brighter still)

Light

Umbra

Penumbra

- **Shadow.** An area which light rays cannot reach due to an obstacle in their path. If the rays come from a point they are stopped by the obstacle, creating a complete shadow called an **umbra**. If they come from an extended source, a semi-shadow area called a **penumbra** is formed around the umbra.

Reflection of light

Reflection is the change in direction of a wave when it bounces off a boundary (see page 36). Mirrors are usually used to show the reflection of light (see right and also pages 48-49). It must be noted that when an object and its image are drawn in mirror (and **lens***) diagrams, the object is assumed to be producing light rays itself. In fact the rays come from a source, e.g. the sun, and have already been reflected once, i.e. off the object.

Incident ray. Ray of light before reflection (or **refraction***).

Angle of incidence (i). Angle between **incident ray** and **normal** at **point of incidence**.

Point of incidence. Point at which **incident ray** meets boundary and becomes **reflected ray** (or **refracted ray***).

Normal. Line at right angles to boundary through chosen point, e.g. **point of incidence**.

Angle of reflection (r). Angle between **reflected ray** and **normal** at **point of incidence**.

Reflected ray

Laws of reflection of light

1. The **reflected ray** lies in the same plane as the **incident ray** and the **normal** at the **point of incidence**.

2. The **angle of incidence (i)** = the **angle of reflection (r)**

- **Regular reflection.** The reflection of parallel **incident rays** (see above) off a flat surface such that all the **reflected rays** are also parallel. This occurs when surfaces are very smooth, e.g. highly polished surfaces such as mirrors.

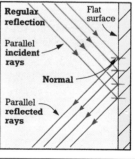

Regular reflection

Flat surface

Parallel incident rays

Normal

Parallel reflected rays

* Electromagnetic waves, 44; Frequency, 35; Lenses, 52; Refracted ray, Refraction, 50; Wavelength, 34.

- **Eclipse.** The total or partial "blocking off" of light from a source. This occurs when an object casts a **shadow** by passing between the source and an observer. A **solar eclipse** is seen from the earth when the moon passes between the earth and the sun, and a **lunar eclipse** is seen when the earth is between the sun and the moon.

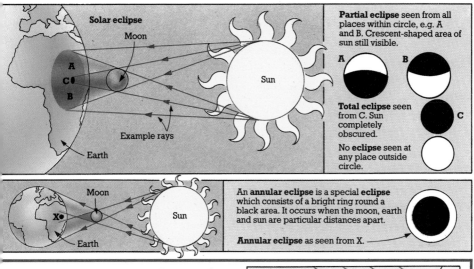

Solar eclipse
Moon
Sun
Example rays
Earth

A
C
B

Partial eclipse seen from all places within circle, e.g. A and B. Crescent-shaped area of sun still visible.

A   B

Total eclipse seen from C. Sun completely obscured.

C

No **eclipse** seen at any place outside circle.

Moon
Sun
Earth
X

An **annular eclipse** is a special **eclipse** which consists of a bright ring round a black area. It occurs when the moon, earth and sun are particular distances apart.

Annular eclipse as seen from X.

- **Diffuse reflection.** The reflection of parallel **incident rays** (see left) off a rough surface such that the **reflected rays** travel in different directions and the light is scattered. This is the most common type of reflection as most surfaces are irregular when considered on a scale comparable to that of the **wavelength*** of light (see page 44).

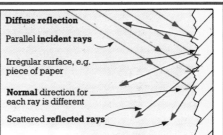

Diffuse reflection

Parallel **incident rays**

Irregular surface, e.g. piece of paper

Normal direction for each ray is different

Scattered **reflected rays**

- **Plane mirror.** A mirror with a flat surface (see also **curved mirrors**, pages 48-49). The image it forms is the same size as the object, the same distance behind ("inside") the mirror as the object is in front, and **laterally inverted** (the left and right sides have swapped round).

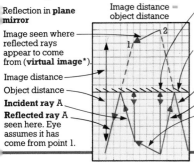

Reflection in **plane mirror**

Image seen where reflected rays appear to come from (**virtual image***).

Image distance

Object distance

Incident ray A

Reflected ray A seen here. Eye assumes it has come from point 1.

Image distance = object distance

2

1

Rays hitting at right angles are reflected back along same line

Plane mirror

Reflected ray B seen here. Eye assumes it has come from point 2.

Incident ray B

Object (from which light rays are assumed to have originated – see reflection of light, page 46).

- **Parallax.** The apparent movement of two objects relative to one another, as seen by a moving observer. For example, two objects at different distances from a moving train appear to move past each other to someone looking at them from the train window – the further away of the two objects appearing to move faster and hence a greater distance.

* **Virtual image**, 49 (**Image**); **Wavelength**, 34.

Reflection of light (continued)

Light rays are reflected from curved surfaces, as from flat surfaces, according to the **laws of reflection of light** (see page 46). The images formed by reflection from **curved mirrors** are particularly easily observed. There are two types of curved mirror – **concave** and **convex mirrors**. For all diagrams showing reflection of light, the object is assumed to be the source of the light (see **reflection of light**, page 46) and certain points (see below), together with known facts about light rays passing through them, are used to construct the paths of the reflected rays.

Points used to construct paths of reflected rays (see also page 52):

Pole (P). Centre of curved mirror.

Centre of curvature (C). Centre of sphere of which curved mirror is part. Any light ray passing through it (**concave mirrors**) or heading directly for it (**convex mirrors**) reflected back on itself.

Radius of curvature (r). Distance between **centre of curvature** and pole.

Aperture. Area light passes through to hit mirror.

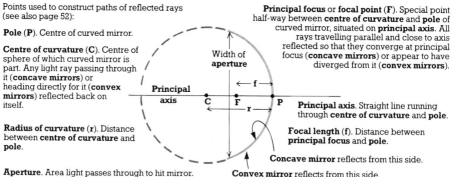

Principal focus or **focal point (F).** Special point half-way between **centre of curvature** and pole of curved mirror, situated on **principal axis**. All rays travelling parallel and close to axis reflected so that they converge at principal focus (**concave mirrors**) or appear to have diverged from it (**convex mirrors**).

Principal axis. Straight line running through **centre of curvature** and pole.

Focal length (f). Distance between **principal focus** and pole.

Concave mirror reflects from this side.

Convex mirror reflects from this side.

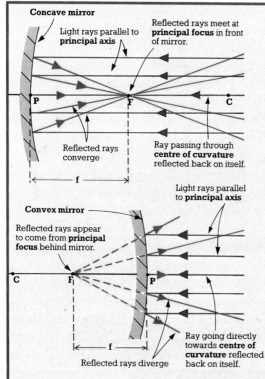

Concave mirror

Light rays parallel to **principal axis**

Reflected rays meet at **principal focus** in front of mirror.

P — F — C

Reflected rays converge

Ray passing through **centre of curvature** reflected back on itself.

f

Convex mirror

Reflected rays appear to come from **principal focus** behind mirror.

C — F — P

Light rays parallel to **principal axis**

f

Reflected rays diverge

Ray going directly towards **centre of curvature** reflected back on itself.

- **Concave** or **converging mirror.** A mirror with a reflecting surface which curves inward (part of the inside of a sphere). When light rays parallel to the **principal axis** fall on such a mirror, they are reflected so that they converge at the **principal focus** in front of the mirror. The size, position and type of **image** formed depends on how far the object is from the mirror.

- **Convex** or **diverging mirror.** A mirror with a reflecting surface which curves outwards (part of the outside of a sphere). When light rays parallel to the **principal axis** fall on such a mirror, they are reflected so that they appear to diverge from the **principal focus** behind ("inside") the mirror. The **images** formed are always upright and reduced, and **virtual images** (see **image**).

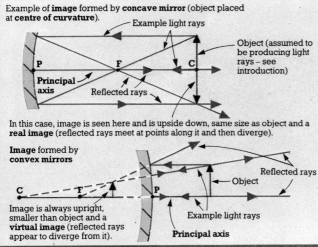

Example of **image** formed by **concave mirror** (object placed at **centre of curvature**).

Example light rays

Object (assumed to be producing light rays – see introduction)

P   F   C

Principal axis

Reflected rays

In this case, image is seen here and is upside down, same size as object and a **real image** (reflected rays meet at points along it and then diverge).

Image formed by **convex mirrors**

Reflected rays

Object

C   F   P

Image is always upright, smaller than object and a **virtual image** (reflected rays appear to diverge from it).

Example light rays

Principal axis

● **Image.** A view of an object at a place other than where the object is. Just as an object is only seen because of light rays coming from it (see **reflection of light**, page 46), so too an image is seen where reflected rays (originally from the object) actually diverge from (**real image**), or appear to diverge from (**virtual image**).

● **Mirror** or **lens formula.** Gives the relationship between the distance of an object from the centre of a curved mirror or **lens***, the distance of its **image** from the same point and the **focal length** of the mirror or lens. An image may be formed either side of a mirror or lens, so a **sign convention*** is used to give position.

Mirror formula:

$$\frac{1}{f} = \frac{1}{v} + \frac{1}{u}$$

where f = **focal length**; v = **image** distance (from **pole**); u = object distance (from pole).

Real is positive sign convention

1. All distances are measured from the mirror as origin.
2. Distances of objects and **real images** are positive.
3. Distances of **virtual images** are negative.

● **Linear magnification.** The ratio of the height of the image formed by a mirror or **lens*** to the object height.

$$\text{Linear magnification} = \frac{\text{height of image}}{\text{height of object}}$$

● **Principle of reversibility of light.** States that, for a ray of light on a given path due to reflection, **refraction*** or **diffraction***, a ray of light in the opposite direction in the same conditions will follow the same path. Light rays parallel to the **principal axis**, for example, are reflected by a **concave mirror** to meet at the **principal focus**. If a point source of light is placed at the principal focus, the rays are reflected parallel to the axis.

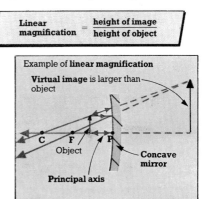

Example of **linear magnification**

Virtual image is larger than object

C   F   P

Object

Concave mirror

Principal axis

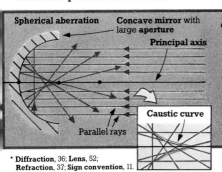

Spherical aberration   Concave mirror with large **aperture**

Principal axis

Caustic curve

Parallel rays

● **Spherical aberration.** An effect seen when rays parallel to the **principal axis** (and different distances from it), hit a curved mirror and are reflected so that they intersect at different points along the axis, forming a **caustic curve**. The larger the **aperture**, the more this is seen. It is also seen in **lenses*** with large apertures.

* **Diffraction**, 36; **Lens**, 52; **Refraction**, 37; **Sign convention**, 11.

Refraction of light

Refraction is the change in direction of any wave as a result of its velocity changing when it moves from one **medium*** into another (see also page 37). When light rays (see page 46) move into a new medium, they are refracted according to the **laws of refraction of light**. The direction in which they are refracted depends on whether they move into a denser or less dense medium and are consequently slowed down or speeded up (see diagram below).

Refraction at boundary between two **media***

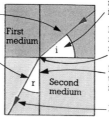

Incident ray. Ray of light before refraction (or **reflection***)

Angle of refraction (r). Angle between **refracted ray** and **normal** at **point of incidence**.

If second medium denser, ray slows down and is refracted towards **normal** as here. If less dense, ray speeds up and is refracted away from normal.

First medium

Second medium

Angle of incidence (i). Angle between incident ray and normal at point of incidence.

Point of incidence. Point at which **incident ray** meets boundary and becomes **refracted ray** (or **reflected ray***).

Normal. Line at right angles to boundary through chosen point, e.g. **point of incidence**.

Refracted ray

Laws of refraction of light

1. The **refracted ray** lies in the same plane as the **incident ray** and **normal** at the **point of incidence**.

2. **(Snell's law)**. The ratio of the **sine*** of the **angle of incidence** to the sine of the **angle of refraction** is a constant for two given **media***. This constant is the **refractive index (n** – see page 37). When referring to light, this is also known as the **optical density** and, as with refractive index in other cases, can also be calculated by dividing the velocity of light in one medium by its velocity in the second medium. See also **apparent depth** picture.

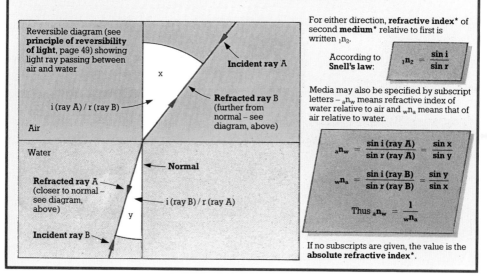

Reversible diagram (see **principle of reversibility of light**, page 49) showing light ray passing between air and water

x

i (ray A) / r (ray B)

Air

Water

Refracted ray A (closer to normal – see diagram, above)

Incident ray B

y

Incident ray A

Refracted ray B (further from normal – see diagram, above)

Normal

i (ray B) / r (ray A)

For either direction, **refractive index*** of second **medium*** relative to first is written $_1n_2$.

According to Snell's law:

$$_1n_2 = \frac{\sin i}{\sin r}$$

Media may also be specified by subscript letters – $_an_w$ means refractive index of water relative to air and $_wn_a$ means that of air relative to water.

$$_an_w = \frac{\sin i \text{ (ray A)}}{\sin r \text{ (ray A)}} = \frac{\sin x}{\sin y}$$

$$_wn_a = \frac{\sin i \text{ (ray B)}}{\sin r \text{ (ray B)}} = \frac{\sin y}{\sin x}$$

$$\text{Thus } _an_w = \frac{1}{_wn_a}$$

If no subscripts are given, the value is the **absolute refractive index***.

* Absolute refractive index, 37 (Refractive index); Medium, 115; Reflected ray, Reflection, 46; Sine, 115.

- **Apparent depth**. The position at which an object in one **medium*** appears to be when viewed from another medium. The brain assumes the light rays have travelled in a straight line, but in fact they have changed direction as a result of refraction. Hence the object is not actually where it appears to be.

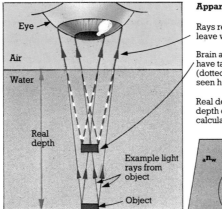

Apparent depth

Rays refracted when they leave water

Brain assumes light rays have taken straight paths (dotted lines), so object seen here.

Real depth and apparent depth can also be used to calculate **refractive index***:

Eye

Air

Water

Real depth

Example light rays from object

Object

$$_an_w = \frac{\text{real depth}}{\text{apparent depth}}$$

$$\left(_wn_a = \frac{1}{_an_w} \right)$$

- **Critical angle (c)**. The particular **angle of incidence** of a ray hitting a less dense **medium*** which results in it being refracted at 90° to the **normal**. ▶ This means that the refracted ray (**critical ray**) travels along the boundary, and does not enter the second medium.

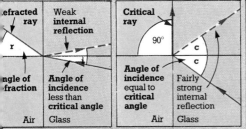

Refracted ray	Weak internal reflection	Critical ray		Total internal reflection	
r		90°			i
i		c / c			
Angle of refraction	Angle of incidence less than critical angle	Angle of incidence equal to critical angle	Fairly strong internal reflection	Angle of incidence greater than critical angle	
Air	Glass	Air	Glass	Air	Glass

Critical angle can also be used to calculate **refractive index***:

$$_gn_a = \sin c$$

$$\left(_an_g = \frac{1}{_gn_a} \right)$$

(Note: sine of 90° is 1)

- **Total internal reflection**. When light travelling from a dense to a less dense **medium*** hits the boundary between them, some degree of reflection back into the denser medium (**internal reflection**) always accompanies ▶ refraction. When the **angle of incidence** is greater than the **critical angle**, total internal reflection occurs, i.e. all the light is internally reflected.

Optical fibres transmit light by **total internal reflection**. Bundles of such fibres have a number of uses, e.g. in communications and in medicine (e.g. in **endoscopes**, used by doctors to see inside the body)

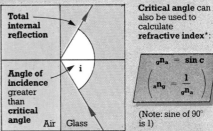

Glass fibre Light rays

Outer layer of less dense glass

Bundle of fibres

Angle of incidence greater than **critical angle**, so **total internal reflection** occurs.

- **Prism**. A transparent solid which has two plane refracting surfaces at an angle to each other. Prisms are used to produce **dispersion*** and change the path of light by refraction and **total internal reflection**.

Prism refracting light ray

Angle of deviation, i.e. angle between ray entering prism and ray emerging from it.

Path of ray if it had not passed through prism.

Prism causing **total internal reflection**

Angle of incidence greater than **critical angle**

Angle of deviation = 90°

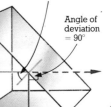

Refraction of light (continued)

Light rays are refracted at curved surfaces, e.g. **lenses**, as at flat surfaces, according to the **laws of refraction of light** (see page 50). Unlike with flat surfaces, though, images are formed. There are two basic types of lens, **concave** and **convex lenses**, which can act as **diverging** or **converging lenses** depending on their **refractive index*** relative to the surrounding **medium***. For all diagrams showing image production by refraction, the object is assumed to be the light source (see **reflection of light**, page 46), and certain points (see below), together with known facts about light rays passing through them, are used to construct the paths of the refracted rays. The positions of objects and images can be determined using the **mirror (lens) formula***.

Points used to construct paths of refracted rays (see also page 48). All lenses shown are considered thin lenses (i.e. thickness of lens small compared to **focal length**). Though rays bend both on entering and emerging, they are drawn as bending only once, at a vertical line running through **optical centre**.

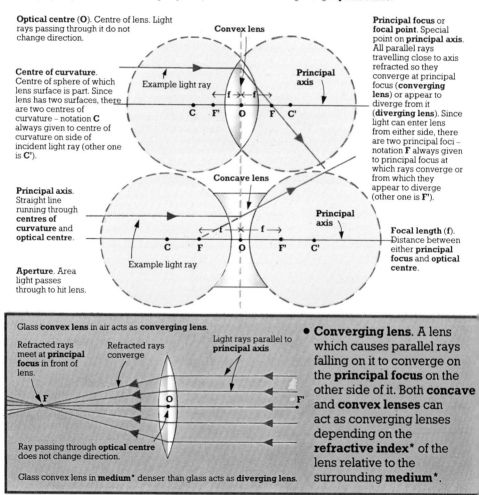

Optical centre (O). Centre of lens. Light rays passing through it do not change direction.

Centre of curvature. Centre of sphere of which lens surface is part. Since lens has two surfaces, there are two centres of curvature – notation **C** always given to centre of curvature on side of incident light ray (other one is **C'**).

Principal axis. Straight line running through centres of curvature and optical centre.

Aperture. Area light passes through to hit lens.

Convex lens

Example light ray

Principal axis

Concave lens

Example light ray

Principal axis

Principal focus or **focal point.** Special point on **principal axis**. All parallel rays travelling close to axis refracted so they converge at principal focus (**converging lens**) or appear to diverge from it (**diverging lens**). Since light can enter lens from either side, there are two principal foci – notation **F** always given to principal focus at which rays converge or from which they appear to diverge (other one is **F'**).

Focal length (f). Distance between either **principal focus** and optical centre.

Glass convex lens in air acts as converging lens.

Refracted rays meet at **principal focus** in front of lens.

Refracted rays converge

Light rays parallel to **principal axis**

Ray passing through **optical centre** does not change direction.

Glass convex lens in **medium*** denser than glass acts as **diverging lens.**

• **Converging lens.** A lens which causes parallel rays falling on it to converge on the **principal focus** on the other side of it. Both **concave** and **convex lenses** can act as converging lenses depending on the **refractive index*** of the lens relative to the surrounding **medium***.

* **Medium**, 115; **Mirror formula**, 49; **Refractive index**, 37.

- **Convex lens.** A lens with at least one surface curving outwards. A lens with one surface curving inwards and one outwards is convex if its middle is thicker than its outer edges (it is a **convex meniscus**). A glass convex lens in air acts as a **converging lens**. The size, position and type of image it forms (**real*** or **virtual***) depends on how far it is from the object.

Types of convex lens

Bi-convex

Plano-convex

Convex meniscus

- **Concave lens.** A lens which has at least one surface curving inwards. A lens with one surface curving inwards and one outwards is concave if its middle is thinner than its outer edges (it is a **concave meniscus**). A glass concave lens in air acts as a **diverging lens**. The position of the object in relation to the lens may vary, but the image is always of the same type.

Types of concave lens

Bi-concave

Plano-concave

Concave meniscus

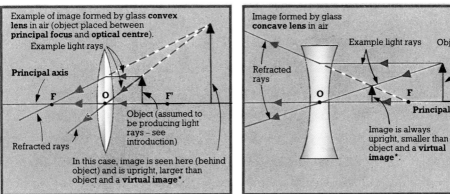

Example of image formed by glass **convex lens** in air (object placed between **principal focus** and **optical centre**).

Example light rays

Principal axis

F O F'

Refracted rays

Object (assumed to be producing light rays – see introduction)

In this case, image is seen here (behind object) and is upright, larger than object and a **virtual image***.

Image formed by glass **concave lens** in air

Example light rays Object

Refracted rays

O F

Principal axis

Image is always upright, smaller than object and a **virtual image***.

- **Power (P).** A measure of the ability of a lens to converge or diverge light rays, given in **dioptres** (when **focal length** is measured in metres). The shorter the focal length, the more powerful the lens.

$$P = \frac{1}{f}$$

where P = **power** of lens; f = **focal length**.

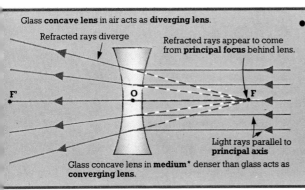

Glass **concave lens** in air acts as **diverging lens**.

Refracted rays diverge

Refracted rays appear to come from **principal focus** behind lens.

F' O F

Light rays parallel to **principal axis**

Glass concave lens in **medium*** denser than glass acts as **converging lens**.

- **Diverging lens.** A lens which causes parallel rays falling on it to diverge so that they appear to have come from the **principal focus** on the same side as the rays enter. Both **concave** and **convex lenses** can act as diverging lenses, depending on the **refractive index*** of the lens relative to the surrounding **medium***.

* Medium, 115; Real image, 49 (Image); Refractive index, 37; Virtual image, 49 (Image).

Optical instruments

An **optical instrument** is one which acts on light, using one or more **lenses*** or **curved mirrors*** to produce a required type of image. Listed below are some of the more common optical instruments.

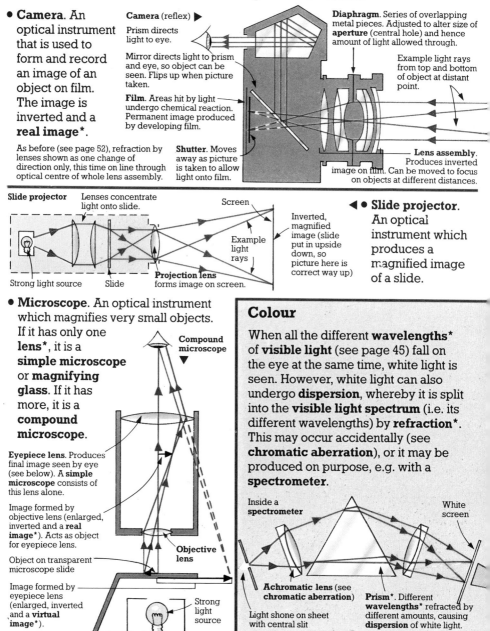

- **Camera.** An optical instrument that is used to form and record an image of an object on film. The image is inverted and a **real image***.

As before (see page 52), refraction by lenses shown as one change of direction only, this time through optical centre of whole lens assembly.

Camera (reflex) ▶

Prism directs light to eye.

Mirror directs light to prism and eye, so object can be seen. Flips up when picture taken.

Film. Areas hit by light undergo chemical reaction. Permanent image produced by developing film.

Shutter. Moves away as picture is taken to allow light onto film.

Diaphragm. Series of overlapping metal pieces. Adjusted to alter size of **aperture** (central hole) and hence amount of light allowed through.

Example light rays from top and bottom of object at distant point.

Lens assembly. Produces inverted image on film. Can be moved to focus on objects at different distances.

Slide projector

Lenses concentrate light onto slide.

Strong light source

Slide

Projection lens forms image on screen.

Screen

Example light rays

Inverted, magnified image (slide put in upside down, so picture here is correct way up)

◀ • **Slide projector.** An optical instrument which produces a magnified image of a slide.

- **Microscope.** An optical instrument which magnifies very small objects. If it has only one **lens***, it is a **simple microscope** or **magnifying glass**. If it has more, it is a **compound microscope**.

Compound microscope ▼

Eyepiece lens. Produces final image seen by eye (see below). A **simple microscope** consists of this lens alone.

Image formed by objective lens (enlarged, inverted and a **real image***). Acts as object for eyepiece lens.

Object on transparent microscope slide

Image formed by eyepiece lens (enlarged, inverted and a **virtual image***).

Objective lens

Strong light source

Colour

When all the different **wavelengths*** of **visible light** (see page 45) fall on the eye at the same time, white light is seen. However, white light can also undergo **dispersion**, whereby it is split into the **visible light spectrum** (i.e. its different wavelengths) by **refraction***. This may occur accidentally (see **chromatic aberration**), or it may be produced on purpose, e.g. with a **spectrometer**.

Inside a **spectrometer**

White screen

Achromatic lens (see **chromatic aberration**)

Light shone on sheet with central slit

Prism*. Different **wavelengths*** refracted by different amounts, causing **dispersion** of white light.

* **Curved mirrors**, 48; **Lenses**, 52; **Prism**, 51; **Real image**, 49 (**Image**); **Refraction**, 50; **Virtual image**, 49 (**Image**); **Wavelength**, 34.

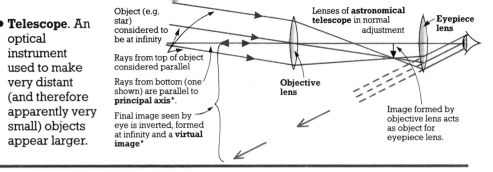

- **Telescope.** An optical instrument used to make very distant (and therefore apparently very small) objects appear larger.

Object (e.g. star) considered to be at infinity

Rays from top of object considered parallel

Rays from bottom (one shown) are parallel to **principal axis***.

Final image seen by eye is inverted, formed at infinity and a **virtual image***

Lenses of **astronomical telescope** in normal adjustment

Eyepiece lens

Objective lens

Image formed by objective lens acts as object for eyepiece lens.

- **Visual angle.** The angle, at the eye, of the rays coming from the top and bottom of an object or its image. The greater it is, the larger the object or image appears. Optical instruments which produce magnification, e.g. **microscopes**, do so by creating an image whose visual angle is greater than that of the object seen by the unaided eye. The **angular magnification** or **magnifying power** (see below) of such an instrument is a measurement of the amount by which it does so.

$$\text{Angular magnification} = \frac{\text{visual angle of image}}{\text{visual angle of object}}$$

- **Chromatic aberration** or **chromatism**. The halo of colours (the **visible light spectrum** – see below, left) sometimes seen around images viewed through lenses. It results from **dispersion** (see **colour**). To avoid this, good quality optical instruments contain one or more **achromatic lenses** – each consisting of two lenses combined so that any dispersion produced by one is corrected by the other.

- **Visible light spectrum.** A display of the colours that make up a beam of white light. Each colour band represents a very small range of **wavelengths*** – see **visible light**, page 45.

Face-on view

Visible light spectrum ▼

- Red
- Orange
- Yellow
- Green
- Blue
- Indigo
- Violet

Primary colours

△ = **secondary colours** (combinations of primary colours)

Complementary colours are any two that produce white light when mixed, e.g. red and cyan.

Red Green

△ Yellow

△ Cyan

Blue △ Magenta

- **Primary colours.** Red, blue and green light – colours that cannot be made by combining other coloured light. Mixed equally, they give white light. By mixing them in the right proportions, every colour in the **visible light spectrum** can be produced. Note these are the pure primary colours – those referred to in art (red, blue and yellow) only act as primary colours because the paints are impure.

- **Colour mixing.** If white light is shone onto a pure coloured filter, only light of the same colour (range of **wavelengths***) as the filter passes through (the other colours are absorbed). This is **subtractive mixing** or **colour mixing by subtraction**. If light of two different colours, filtered out in this way, is shone onto a white surface, a third colour (a mixture of the two) is seen by the eye. This is **additive mixing**, or **colour mixing by addition**.

* **Principal axis**, 52; **Virtual image**, 49 (**Image**); **Wavelength**, 34.

Static electricity

Electricity is the phenomenon caused by the presence or movement of electrically charged particles (**electrons*** or **ions***) which exert an **electric force***. A material is said to have a negative electric charge if it has a surplus of electrons, and a positive charge if it has a deficit of electrons. An electric **current** (see page 60) is the movement of electrons through materials and is therefore a transfer of charge – this can be contrasted with **static electricity**, which can be said to be electricity "held" by a material with electric charge.

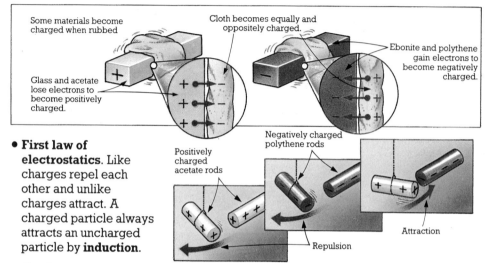

Some materials become charged when rubbed

Cloth becomes equally and oppositely charged.

Glass and acetate lose electrons to become positively charged.

Ebonite and polythene gain electrons to become negatively charged.

- **First law of electrostatics**. Like charges repel each other and unlike charges attract. A charged particle always attracts an uncharged particle by **induction**.

Positively charged acetate rods

Negatively charged polythene rods

Repulsion

Attraction

- **Conductor**. A material containing a large number of electrons which are free to move (see also **conductivity**, page 62). It can therefore **conduct** electricity (carry an electric **current** – see introduction). Good conductors are metals, e.g. copper, aluminium and gold.

- **Insulator**. A material with very few or no electrons free to move (i.e. a bad **conductor**). Some insulators become electrically charged when rubbed because electrons from the surface atoms are transferred from one substance to the next, but the charge remains on the surface.

- **Electroscope**. An instrument for detecting small amounts of electric charge. A **gold leaf electroscope** is the most common type. When the leaf and rod become charged, they repel and the leaf diverges from the rod. The greater the charges, the larger the divergence of the leaf. A **condensing electroscope** contains a **capacitor*** between the cap and the case which increases the sensitivity.

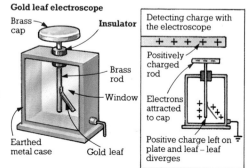

Gold leaf electroscope

Brass cap

Insulator

Brass rod

Window

Earthed metal case

Gold leaf

Detecting charge with the electroscope

+ + + + +

Positively charged rod

Electrons attracted to cap

Positive charge left on plate and leaf – leaf diverges

* Capacitor, 59; Electric force, 6; Electrons, 83; Ions, 88 (Ionization).

- **Induction** or **electrostatic induction**. A process by which a **conductor** becomes charged with the use of another charge but without contact. Generally charges are induced in different parts of an object because of repulsion and attraction. By removing one type of charge the object is left permanently charged.

- **Proof plane**. A small disc made of a **conductor** mounted on a handle made of an **insulator**. It is used to transfer charge between objects.

- **Surface density**. The amount of charge per unit area on the surface of an object. It is greater where the surface is more curved, which leads to charge being concentrated at sharp points (see **point action**). Only a sphere has constant surface density.

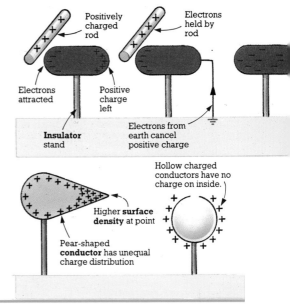

Charging a **conductor** by induction

Positively charged rod

Electrons held by rod

Electrons attracted

Positive charge left

Electrons from earth cancel positive charge

Insulator stand

Hollow charged conductors have no charge on inside.

Higher **surface density** at point

Pear-shaped **conductor** has unequal charge distribution

- **Point action**. The action which occurs around a sharp point on the surface of a positively-charged object. Positive ions in the air are repelled by the large charge at the point (see **surface density**). These collide with air molecules and knock off electrons to produce more positive ions which are also repelled. The result is an **electric wind** of air molecules.

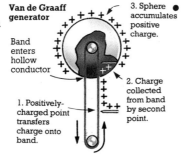

Action of **lightning conductor**

Negatively charged cloud

Electrons repelled to earth by cloud to leave positive charge on point of conductor

Point action causes positive ions in air to move towards cloud, which helps neutralize charge in cloud

Positive charge on point attracts electrons when **lightning** occurs so that current flows down conductor.

- **Lightning**. The sudden flow of electricity from a cloud which has become charged due to the rubbing together of different particles, e.g. water droplets. A **lightning conductor** is used to help cancel the charge on the cloud by **point action** and to conduct the electricity down to earth so it does not flow through buildings. The lightning stroke is like the effect in a **discharge tube***.

- **Van de Graaff generator**. A machine in which positive charge from a point is transferred (by **point action**) to a moving band, collected by another point and deposited on a sphere-shaped conductor.

Van de Graaff generator

Band enters hollow conductor

1. Positively-charged point transfers charge onto band.

2. Charge collected from band by second point.

3. Sphere accumulates positive charge.

- **Electrophorus**. An instrument consisting of a negatively-charged **insulator** and a brass plate on an insulating handle. It is used to produce a number of positive charges from one negative charge.

* **Discharge tube**, 80; **Mechanical energy**, 9.

Potential and capacitance

A difference in charge between any points causes an **electric field**, i.e. a **force field*** in which charged particles experience an **electric force***. The intensity of an electric field at a point is the force per unit positive charge at that point and the direction is the direction of the force at that point (see also pages 104-107). Charged objects in an electric field have **potential energy*** because of their charge and position. **Potential** itself is a property of the field (see below).

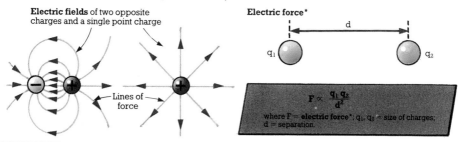

Electric fields of two opposite charges and a single point charge

Lines of force

Electric force*

$$F \propto \frac{q_1 q_2}{d^2}$$

where F = electric force*; q_1, q_2 = size of charges; d = separation.

● **Potential**. The **potential energy*** per unit charge at a point in an electric field, i.e. the work done in moving unit positive charge to this point. The potential energy of a charge depends on the potential of its position and on its size. A positive charge tends to move towards points of lower potential. This is moving down the **potential gradient**. Potential cannot be measured, but the **potential difference** between two points can.

▼

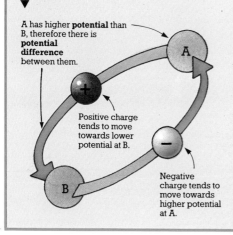

A has higher **potential** than B, therefore there is **potential difference** between them.

Positive charge tends to move towards lower potential at B.

Negative charge tends to move towards higher potential at A.

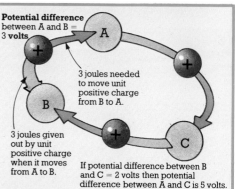

Potential difference between A and B = 3 **volts**

3 joules needed to move unit positive charge from B to A.

3 joules given out by unit positive charge when it moves from A to B.

If potential difference between B and C = 2 volts then potential difference between A and C is 5 volts.

▲

● **Potential difference**. A difference in **potential** between two points, equal to the energy change when a unit positive charge moves from one place to another in an electric field. The unit of potential difference is the **volt** (potential difference is sometimes called **voltage**). There is an energy change of one joule if a charge of one **coulomb*** moves through one volt. A reference point (usually a connection to the earth) is chosen and given a potential of zero.

● **Equipotential**. A surface over which the **potential** is constant.

* Coulomb, 60; Electric force, Force field, Gravitational force, 6; Potential energy, 8.

Capacitance

When a **conductor*** is given a charge it undergoes a change in **potential**. **Capacitance** or **capacity** is the ratio of the charge gained by an object to its increase in potential. An object with a higher capacitance requires a larger charge to change its potential by the same amount as an object with a smaller capacitance.

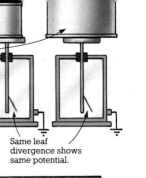

Two different metal cans have different **capacitance**.

More charge (Q) must be given to larger can to give it same **potential**(V) – it has higher capacitance.

Same leaf divergence shows same potential.

Farad. The unit of capacitance. It is the capacitance of an object whose **potential** is increased by one **volt** when given a charge of one **coulomb***.

$$C = \frac{Q}{V}$$

where C = **capacitance**; Q = charge; V = **potential**.

● **Capacitor**. A device for storing electric charge, consisting of two parallel metal plates separated by an insulating material called a **dielectric**. The capacitance of a capacitor depends on the dielectric used, so one is chosen to suit the capacitance needed and the physical size required.

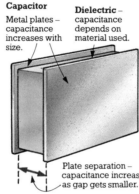

Capacitor
Metal plates – capacitance increases with size.

Dielectric – capacitance depends on material used.

Plate separation – capacitance increases as gap gets smaller.

● **Dielectric constant**. The ratio of the capacitance of a **capacitor** with a given **dielectric** to the capacitance of the same capacitor with a vacuum between the plates. The value is thus the factor by which the capacitance is increased by using the given dielectric instead of a vacuum (note that air is almost the same).

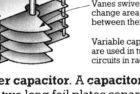

Variable capacitor

Vanes swivel to change area between them.

Variable capacitors are used in tuning circuits in radios.

● **Variable capacitor**. A **capacitor** consisting of two sets of interlocking vanes, often with an air **dieletric**. The size of the interlocking area is altered to change the capacitance.

● **Paper capacitor**. A **capacitor** made ▶ with two long foil plates separated by a thin waxed paper **dielectric**. **Polyester capacitors** are made in a similar way.

Paper or **polyester capacitor**

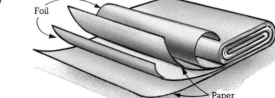

Foil

Paper

● **Electrolytic capacitor**. A **capacitor** with a paste or jelly **dieletric** which gives it a very high capacitance in a small volume. Due to the nature of the dielectric, it must be connected the correct way round to the electricity supply.

● **Leyden jar**. A **capacitor** consisting of a glass jar with foil linings inside and out. It was one of the first capacitors invented.

Electric current

An electric **current** (**I**) is the rate of flow of electric charge. In metal conductors, the charge which flows consists of electrons (negatively-charged particles – see page 83), and these flow because an **electric field*** creates a difference in **potential*** between two places. Therefore a **potential difference*** is needed to produce an electric current. A **circuit** is a closed loop, consisting of a source of current and one or more components, around which current flows.

- **Electromotive force** ▶ (**e.m.f.**). The **potential difference*** produced by a **cell***, **battery*** or **generator***, which causes current to flow in a circuit. A source of e.m.f. has two **terminals** (where wires are connected), between which it maintains a potential difference. A **back e.m.f.** is an e.m.f. produced by a component in the circuit which opposes the main e.m.f.

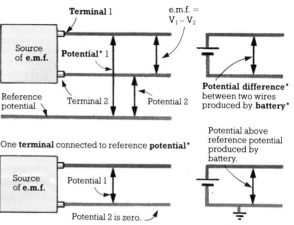

Terminal 1

e.m.f. = $V_1 - V_2$

Source of **e.m.f.**

Potential* 1

Reference potential

Terminal 2

Potential 2

Potential difference* between two wires produced by **battery***

Potential above reference potential produced by battery.

One **terminal** connected to reference **potential***

Source of **e.m.f.**

Potential 1

Potential 2

Potential 2 is zero.

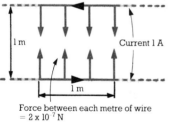

1 m

Current 1 A

1 m

Force between each metre of wire = 2×10^{-7} N

- **Ampere** or **amp** (**A**). The **SI unit*** of current. One ampere is the current which, when flowing through two infinitely long wires one metre apart in a vacuum, produces a force of 2×10^{-7} newtons per metre of wire (see also page 96). Current is accurately measured by a **current balance**, which measures (by adapting the theory above) the force between two coils of wire through which current is flowing. **Ammeters*** are **calibrated*** using current balances.

- **Coulomb**. The **SI unit*** of electric ▶ charge. It is equal to the amount of charge which passes a point in a conductor if one **ampere** flows through the conductor for one second.

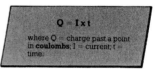

$$Q = I \times t$$

where Q = charge past a point in **coulombs**; I = current; t = time.

- **Direct current** (**d.c.**). Current which flows in one direction only. Originally current was assumed to flow from a point with higher **potential*** to a point with lower potential. Electrons actually flow the other way, but the convention has been kept.

Cell* or **battery*** provides e.m.f. and causes **direct current** to flow.

Current is said to flow from high **potential*** to low potential.

+   −

Electrons flow from point of low potential (negative **terminal**) to point of high potential (positive **terminal**).

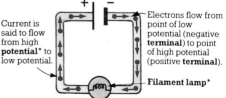

Filament lamp*

* **Ammeter**, 77; **Battery**, 68; **Calibration**, 115; **Cell**, 68; **Electric field**, 58; **Filament lamp**, 64; **Generator**, 78; **Potential, Potential difference**, 58; **SI units**, 96.

- **Alternating current (a.c.).** Current whose direction in a circuit changes at regular intervals. It is caused by an alternating **electromotive force**. Plotting a graph of current against time gives the waveform of the current. Alternating currents and electromotive forces are generally expressed as their **root mean square** values (see picture, right).

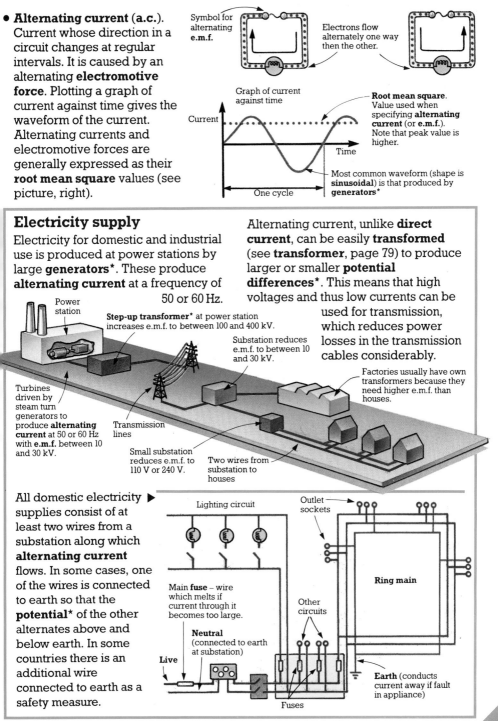

Symbol for alternating **e.m.f.**

Electrons flow alternately one way then the other.

Graph of current against time

Current

Time

One cycle

Root mean square. Value used when specifying **alternating current** (or **e.m.f.**). Note that peak value is higher.

Most common waveform (shape is **sinusoidal**) is that produced by **generators***

Electricity supply

Electricity for domestic and industrial use is produced at power stations by large **generators***. These produce **alternating current** at a frequency of 50 or 60 Hz.

Alternating current, unlike **direct current**, can be easily **transformed** (see **transformer**, page 79) to produce larger or smaller **potential differences***. This means that high voltages and thus low currents can be used for transmission, which reduces power losses in the transmission cables considerably.

Power station

Step-up transformer* at power station increases e.m.f. to between 100 and 400 kV.

Substation reduces e.m.f. to between 10 and 30 kV.

Factories usually have own transformers because they need higher e.m.f. than houses.

Turbines driven by steam turn generators to produce **alternating current** at 50 or 60 Hz with **e.m.f.** between 10 and 30 kV.

Transmission lines

Small substation reduces e.m.f. to 110 V or 240 V.

Two wires from substation to houses

All domestic electricity ▶ supplies consist of at least two wires from a substation along which **alternating current** flows. In some cases, one of the wires is connected to earth so that the **potential*** of the other alternates above and below earth. In some countries there is an additional wire connected to earth as a safety measure.

Lighting circuit

Outlet sockets

Ring main

Main **fuse** – wire which melts if current through it becomes too large.

Other circuits

Neutral (connected to earth at substation)

Live

Fuses

Earth (conducts current away if fault in appliance)

* Generator, 78; Potential, Potential difference, 58; Step-up transformer, 79.

Controlling current

The strength of a current flowing in a circuit depends on the nature of the components in the circuit as well as the **electromotive force***. The **resistance** of the components and the magnetic and electric fields they set up all affect the current in them.

- **Ohm's law.** The current in an object at constant temperature is proportional to the **potential difference*** across its ends. The ratio of the potential difference to the current is the **resistance** of the object. The object must·be at constant temperature for the law to apply since a current will heat it up and this will change its resistance (see also **filament lamp**, page 64). Ohm's law does not apply to some materials, e.g. **semiconductors***.

- **Resistance (R).** The ability of an object to resist the flow of current. The value depends on the **resistivity** of the substance from which the object is made and its shape. The unit of resistance is the **ohm (Ω)**. Electrons moving in the object hit atoms and give them energy, heating the object and using up energy from the source of **electromotive force***.

- **Resistivity (ρ).** The ability of a substance to resist current. Good **conductors*** have a low resistivity and **insulators*** have a high resistivity. It is the **reciprocal*** of the **conductivity** of the substance and depends on temperature. See also page 114.

- **Resistor.** A device with particular **resistance** value, used to produce a required **potential difference***. Resistors can have values from less ▶ than one **ohm** up to many millions of ohms. The most common type is the **carbon resistor**, made from compressed carbon of known **resistivity**.

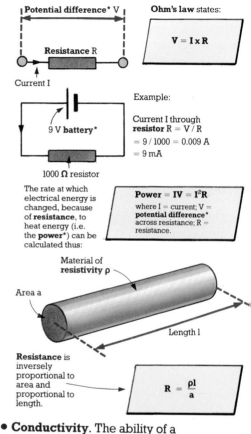

| Potential difference* V |
| Resistance R |
| Current I |

Ohm's law states:

$$V = I \times R$$

Example:

Current I through **resistor** R = V / R
= 9 / 1000 = 0.009 A
= 9 mA

9 V **battery***

1000 Ω resistor

The rate at which electrical energy is changed, because of **resistance**, to heat energy (i.e. the **power***) can be calculated thus:

$$Power = IV = I^2R$$

where I = current; V = **potential difference*** across resistance; R = resistance.

Material of **resistivity** ρ

Area a

Length l

Resistance is inversely proportional to area and proportional to length.

$$R = \frac{\rho l}{a}$$

- **Conductivity.** The ability of a substance to allow the flow of current (see also **conductor** and **insulator**, page 56). It is the inverse of the **resistivity**.

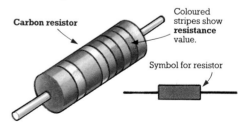

Carbon resistor

Coloured stripes show **resistance** value.

Symbol for resistor

* **Battery**, 68; **Conductor**, 56; **Electromotive force**, 60; **Insulator**, 56; **Potential difference**, 58; **Power**, 9; **Reciprocal**, 115; **Semiconductors**, 65.

Internal resistance (r). The resistance of a **cell*** or **battery*** to the current it causes. It is the resistance of the connections in the cell and some chemical effects (e.g. **polarization***). The current in a circuit may therefore be less than expected.

Internal resistance is part of resistance of circuit.

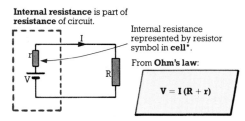

Internal resistance represented by resistor symbol in **cell***.

From **Ohm's law**:

$$V = I\,(R + r)$$

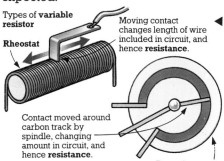

Types of **variable resistor**

Rheostat

Moving contact changes length of wire included in circuit, and hence **resistance**.

Contact moved around carbon track by spindle, changing amount in circuit, and hence **resistance**.

Potentiometer

◀ • **Variable resistor.** A device whose **resistance** can be changed mechanically. It is either a coil of wire of a particular **resistivity** around a drum along which a contact moves (for high currents) or a carbon track with a moving contact. A variable resistor can be used as a **potential divider** if an extra contact is added. It is then a **potentiometer**.

Potential divider or **voltage divider**. ▶ A device used to produce a **potential difference*** from another, higher potential difference.

Circuit diagram of **potential divider**

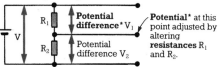

Potential difference* V_1

Potential difference V_2

Potential* at this point adjusted by altering **resistances** R_1 and R_2.

Wheatstone bridge

Unknown resistance

V_A

Galvanometer*

Resistances R_2, R_3 and R_4 adjusted until no current flows through galvanometer.

I_1 I_2

R_1 R_2

R_3 R_4

I_3 I_4

Then $V_A = V_B$, $I_1 = I_2$ and $I_3 = I_4$, and it can be shown that $R_1/R_2 = R_3/R_4$.

V_B

R_1 is then calculated.

◀ • **Wheatstone bridge.** A circuit used to measure an unknown **resistance** (see diagram). When the **galvanometer*** indicates no current, the unknown value of one **resistor** can be calculated from the other three. The **metre bridge** is a version of the wheatstone bridge in which two of the resistors are replaced by a metre of wire with a high resistance. The position of the contact from the galvanometer on the wire gives the ratio R_3/R_4 in the circuit shown.

Kirchhoff's laws. Two laws which ▶ summarize conditions for the flow of current at an instant. The first states that the total current flowing towards a junction is equal to the total current flowing away from the junction. The second states that the sum of the products of **resistance** and current for each component in a circuit is equal to the **electromotive force*** applied to the circuit.

Kirchhoff's first law:

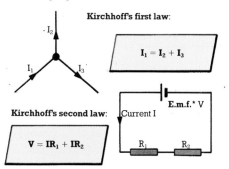

$$I_1 = I_2 + I_3$$

I_1 I_2 I_3

Kirchhoff's second law: Current I

E.m.f.* V

R_1 R_2

$$V = IR_1 + IR_2$$

* Battery, Cell, 68; Electromotive force (e.m.f.), 60; Galvanometer, 77; Polarization, 68; Potential, Potential difference, 58.

Controlling current (continued)

- **Series.** An arrangement of components in which all of the current passes through them one after the other.

- **Parallel.** An arrangement of components in which current divides to pass through all at once.

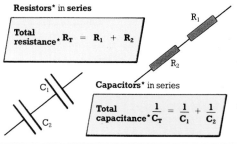

Resistors* in series

| Total resistance* | R_T | $=$ | R_1 | $+$ | R_2 |

Capacitors* in series

Total capacitance* $\dfrac{1}{C_T} = \dfrac{1}{C_1} + \dfrac{1}{C_2}$

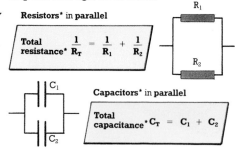

Resistors* in parallel

Total resistance* $\dfrac{1}{R_T} = \dfrac{1}{R_1} + \dfrac{1}{R_2}$

Capacitors* in parallel

Total capacitance* $C_T = C_1 + C_2$

- **Impedance.** The ratio of the **potential difference*** applied to a circuit to the **alternating current*** which flows in it. It is due to two things, the **resistance*** of the circuit and the **reactance**. The effect of impedance is that the **e.m.f.*** and current can be out of phase.

- **Reactance.** The "active" part of **impedance** to **alternating current***. It is caused by **capacitance*** and **inductance** in a circuit which alter the **electromotive forces*** as the current changes.

- **Inductance.** The part of the **impedance** of a circuit due to changing magnetic fields affecting the current (see also **electromagnetic induction**, page 78). This happens in a device called an **inductor**.

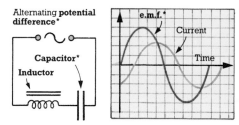

Alternating **potential difference***

Capacitor*

Inductor

- **Filament lamp.** A lamp consisting of a coil of tungsten wire (the **filament**) inside a glass bulb containing argon or nitrogen gas at low pressure. When current flows through the coil, it heats up rapidly and gives out light. Tungsten is used because it has a very high melting point and the bulb is gas-filled to reduce evaporation of the tungsten.

- **Switch.** A device, normally mechanical (but see also **transistor**), which is used to make or break a circuit. A **relay*** is used when a small current is required to switch a larger current on and off.

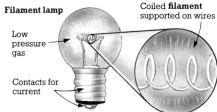

Filament lamp

Coiled **filament** supported on wires

Low pressure gas

Contacts for current

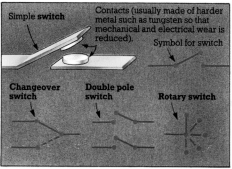

Simple **switch**

Contacts (usually made of harder metal such as tungsten so that mechanical and electrical wear is reduced).

Symbol for switch

Changeover switch

Double pole switch

Rotary switch

* Alternating current, 61; Capacitance, Capacitor, 59; Electromotive force (e.m.f.), 60; Potential difference, 58; Relay, 75; Resistance, Resistor, 62.

Semiconductors

Semiconductors are materials whose **resistivity*** is between that of a **conductor** and an **insulator** (see page 56) and decreases with increasing temperature or increasing amounts of impurities (see **doping**). They are widely used in electronic circuits (see also page 111).

● **Doping.** The introduction of a small amount of impurity into a semiconductor. Depending on the impurity used, the semiconductor is known as either a **p-type** or **n-type**. Combinations of the two types are used to make **diodes** and **transistors**.

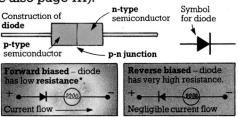

Construction of diode
p-type semiconductor
n-type semiconductor
p-n junction
Symbol for diode

Forward biased – diode has low **resistance***.
Current flow

Reverse biased – diode has very high resistance.
Negligible current flow

● **Diode.** A device made from one piece of **p-type** semiconductor (see **doping**) and one piece of **n-type** semiconductor joined together. It has a very low **resistance*** in one direction (when it is said to be **forward biased**) and a very high resistance in the other direction (**reverse biased**).

● **Half-wave rectification.** The use of a **diode** to remove all the current flowing in one direction from **alternating current***. Current only flows one way around the circuit.

Half-wave rectification

Alternating current* source
Current through resistor*

● **Full-wave rectification.** The conversion of **alternating current*** to **direct current***. It is used when direct current is required from mains electricity.

Full-wave rectification

Alternating current* source
Current through resistor*

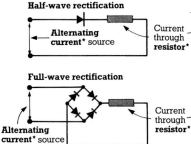

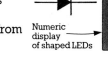

Symbol for **light emitting diode**

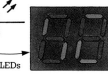

Numeric display of shaped LEDs

● **Light emitting diode (LED).** A **diode** with a higher **resistance*** than normal, in which light is produced instead of heat.

● **Thermistor.** A semiconductor device whose **resistance*** varies with temperature, used to electronically detect temperature changes.

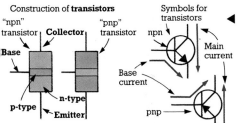

Construction of **transistors**
"npn" transistor
Collector
Base
p-type
n-type
Emitter
"pnp" transistor

Symbols for transistors
npn
Main current
Base current
pnp

● **Transistor.** A semiconductor, normally made from a combination of the two types of semiconductor. There are three connections, the **base**, **collector** and **emitter** (see ◄ diagram). The **resistance*** between the collector and emitter changes from very high to very low when a small current flows into the base. This small base current can therefore be used to control a much larger collector to emitter current.

---

* Alternating current, 61; Direct current, 60; Resistance, Resistivity, Resistor, 62.

Electrolysis

Electrolysis is the process whereby electric current flows through a liquid containing **ions*** (atoms which have gained or lost an **electron*** to become charged) and the liquid is broken down as a result. The current is conducted by the movement of ions in the liquid and chemicals are deposited at the points where the current enters or leaves the liquid. There are a number of industrial applications.

- **Electrolyte.** A compound which conducts electricity when either molten or dissolved in water. All compounds made from ions or which split into ions when dissolved (**ionization***) are electrolytes. The concentration of ions in an electrolyte determines how well it conducts electricity.

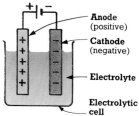

Anode (positive)
Cathode (negative)
Electrolyte
Electrolytic cell

- **Electrode.** A piece of metal or carbon placed in an **electrolyte** through which electric current enters or leaves during electrolysis. Two are needed – the **anode** (positive electrode) and the **cathode** (negative electrode). An **active electrode** is one which is chemically changed by electrolysis; an **inert electrode** is one which is not changed.

- **Electrolytic cell.** A vessel in which electrolysis takes place. It contains the **electrolyte** and the **electrodes**.

- **Ionic theory of electrolysis.** A theory which attempts to explain what happens in the **electrolyte** and at the **electrodes** during electrolysis. It states that the **cations** (positive ions) are attracted towards the **cathode** and the **anions** (negative ions) towards the **anode**. There they lose or gain electrons respectively to form atoms (they are said to be **discharged**). If there are two or more different anions, then one of them will be discharged in preference to the others. This is called **preferential discharge.** ▼

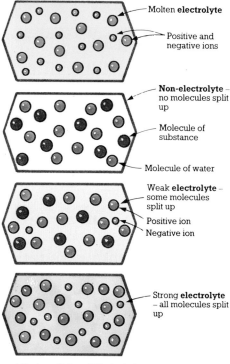

Molten **electrolyte**

Positive and negative ions

Non-electrolyte – no molecules split up

Molecule of substance

Molecule of water

Weak **electrolyte** – some molecules split up

Positive ion
Negative ion

Strong **electrolyte** – all molecules split up

Electrolysis of copper sulphate solution

Anions attracted to **anode**.

Cations attracted to **cathode**.

Hydroxide ions **preferentially discharge**.

Copper ions preferentially discharge.

$4OH^- \rightarrow 4e^- + 2H_2O + O_2$

Carbon electrodes

$Cu^{2+} + 2e^- \rightarrow Cu$

Oxygen bubbles form on anode.

Copper deposited on cathode.

Sulphate ions do not discharge.

Hydrogen ions do not discharge.

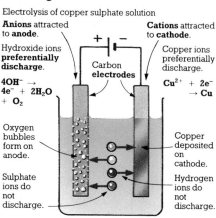

* **Electrons**, 83; **Ions**, 88 (**Ionization**).

Faraday's laws of electrolysis. Two laws which relate the quantity of electricity which passes through an **electrolyte** to the masses of the substances formed. **Faraday's first law** states that the mass of the substances is proportional to the quantity of electricity (the **electrochemical equivalent** of a substance is the mass liberated by one ampere flowing for one second). **Faraday's second law** states that the mass of the substance deposited is inversely proportional to the size of the charge on its ion.

Electrolysis of copper sulphate solution with copper **electrodes (copper voltameter)**

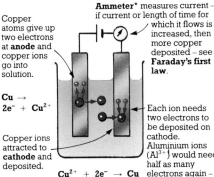

Copper atoms give up two electrons at **anode** and copper ions go into solution.

$$Cu \rightarrow 2e^- + Cu^{2+}$$

Copper ions attracted to **cathode** and deposited.

$$Cu^{2+} + 2e^- \rightarrow Cu$$

Ammeter* measures current – if current or length of time for which it flows is increased, then more copper deposited – see **Faraday's first law**.

Each ion needs two electrons to be deposited on cathode. Aluminium ions (Al^{3+}) would need half as many electrons again – see **Faraday's second law**.

● **Voltameter** or **coulometer.** An **electrolytic cell** used for investigating the relationships between the amount of substance produced at the **electrodes** and the current which passes through the cell. For example, the **copper voltameter** (see below left) contains copper sulphate and copper electrodes.

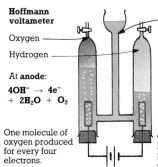

Hoffmann voltameter

Oxygen —
Hydrogen —

Water with small amount of sulphuric acid added (causes more hydrogen and hydroxide ions to be produced to speed up experiment).

At **anode**:
$$4OH^- \rightarrow 4e^- + 2H_2O + O_2$$

At **cathode**:
$$2H^+ + 2e^- \rightarrow H_2$$

One molecule of oxygen produced for every four electrons.

One molecule of hydrogen gas produced for every two electrons.

● **Hoffmann voltameter.** A type of ▲ **voltameter** used for collecting and measuring the volumes (and hence the masses) of gases liberated during electrolysis. For example, electrolysis of acidified water produces hydrogen and oxygen in a two to one ratio (note that this also indicates the chemical composition of water, i.e. H_2O).

Uses of electrolysis

● **Electroplating** or **electrodeposition.** The coating of a metal object with a thin layer of another metal by electrolysis. The object forms the **cathode** and ions of the coating metal are in the **electrolyte**.

Gold and silver plating

Chromium plating (metal normally copper or nickel plated beforehand) stops corrosion.

● **Electro-refining.** A method of purifying metals by electrolysis. Impure metal forms the **anode**, from which metal ions move to the **cathode** and form pure metal. The impurities fall to the bottom of the vessel.

● **Metal extraction.** A process which produces metals from their molten ores by electrolysis. Very reactive metals are obtained by this process, e.g. sodium and aluminium. ▼

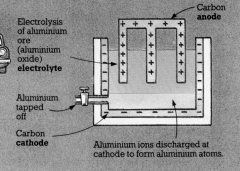

Electrolysis of aluminium ore (aluminium oxide) **electrolyte**

Carbon anode

Aluminium tapped off

Carbon cathode

Aluminium ions discharged at cathode to form aluminium atoms.

Cells and batteries

The Italian scientist Volta first showed that a **potential difference*** exists between two different metals when they are placed in certain liquids (**electrolytes***) and therefore that a **direct current*** can be produced from chemical energy. This arrangement is called a **cell** or **voltaic cell**. The potential difference (caused by chemical changes in the cell) is called an **electromotive force*** and its size depends on the metals used. A **battery** is a number of cells linked together.

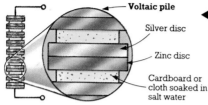

Voltaic pile

Silver disc

Zinc disc

Cardboard or cloth soaked in salt water

◀● **Voltaic pile.** The first battery made, consisting of a pile of silver and zinc discs separated by cardboard or cloth soaked in salt water. This arrangement is the same as a number of **simple cells** linked together.

● **Simple cell.** Two plates of different ▶ metals separated by a salt or acid solution **electrolyte*** (normally copper and zinc plates and dilute sulphuric acid). The simple cell only produces an **electromotive force*** for a short time before **polarization** and **local action** have an effect.

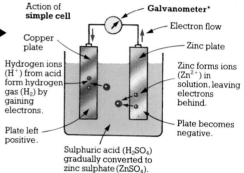

Action of simple cell

Galvanometer*

Electron flow

Copper plate

Zinc plate

Hydrogen ions (H^+) from acid form hydrogen gas (H_2) by gaining electrons.

Zinc forms ions (Zn^{2+}) in solution, leaving electrons behind.

Plate left positive.

Plate becomes negative.

Sulphuric acid (H_2SO_4) gradually converted to zinc sulphate ($ZnSO_4$).

● **Polarization.** The formation of bubbles of hydrogen on the copper plate in a **simple cell**. This reduces the **electromotive force*** of the cell, both because the bubbles insulate the plate and also because a **back e.m.f.*** is set up. Polarization can be eliminated by adding a **depolarizing agent**, which reacts with the hydrogen to form water.

Simple cell

Local action

Impurity in zinc – hydrogen formed because of tiny simple cell.

Polarization

Bubbles of hydrogen gas formed while cell in use.

● **Local action.** The production of hydrogen at the zinc plate in a **simple cell**. Impurities (traces of other metals) in the zinc plate mean that tiny simple cells are formed which produce hydrogen due to **polarization**. Hydrogen is also produced as the zinc dissolves in the acid (even when the cell is not working). Local action can be prevented by coating the plate with an **amalgam** (an alloy of mercury).

* Back e.m.f., 60 (**Electromotive force**); **Direct current**, 60; **Electrolyte**, 66; **Galvanometer**, 77; **Potential difference**, 58.

- **Capacity.** The ability of a cell to produce current over a period of time. It is measured in **ampere hours**. For example, a 10 ampere hour cell should produce one ampere for 10 hours.

- **Leclanché cell.** A cell in which **polarization** is overcome by manganese oxide (a **depolarizing agent**). This removes hydrogen more slowly than it is formed, but continues working to remove excess hydrogen when the cell is not in use. The cell provides an **electromotive force*** of 1.5 V.

Leclanché cell

Zinc rod

Carbon rod

Porous pot

Carbon and manganese oxide (**depolarizing agent**)

Ammonium chloride solution

- **Standard cell.** A cell which produces an accurately known and constant **electromotive force***. It is used in laboratories for experimental work.

- **Primary cell.** Any cell which has a limited life because the chemicals inside it are eventually used up and cannot be replaced easily.

- **Dry cell.** A version of the **Leclanché cell** in which the ammonium chloride solution is replaced by paste containing ammonium chloride, meaning that it is portable. The cell provides an **electromotive force*** of 1.5 V. Dry cells deteriorate slowly due to **local action**, but still have a life of many months.

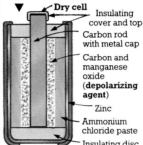

Dry cell

Insulating cover and top

Carbon rod with metal cap

Carbon and manganese oxide (**depolarizing agent**)

Zinc

Ammonium chloride paste

Insulating disc

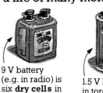

9 V battery (e.g. in radio) is six **dry cells** in **series***

1.5 V battery (e.g. in torch) is one dry cell

- **Secondary cell.** Also known as an **accumulator** or **storage cell**. A cell which can be recharged by connection to another source of electricity. The main types are the **lead-acid accumulator** and the **alkaline cell**.

- **Lead-acid accumulator.** A **secondary cell** containing a dilute sulphuric acid **electrolyte***, and plates made from lead and lead compounds.

- **Alkaline cell.** A **secondary cell** containing an **electrolyte*** of caustic potash solution. The plates are normally made of nickel and cadmium compounds (it is then called a **nickel-cadmium cell**).

The cell can give out a very large current because it has a low **internal resistance***, and is therefore mainly used in vehicles for starting and lighting.

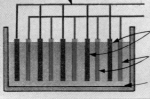

Battery consisting of **lead-acid accumulators**

Plates have large surface area to increase current

Electromotive force* about 2 V

Lead oxide plates (converted to lead sulphate during discharge)

Lead plates (converted to lead sulphate during discharge)

Sulphuric acid (concentration decreases during discharge)

12 V battery (e.g. car battery) consists of six **lead-acid accumulators** in **series***

---

* **Electromotive force**, 60; **Electrolyte**, 66; **Internal resistance**, 63; **Series**, 64.

Magnets

All **magnets** have a **magnetic field*** around them, and a **magnetic force*** exists between two magnets due to the interaction of their fields. Any material which is capable of being **magnetized** (can become a magnet) is described as **magnetic** (see **ferromagnetic**) and becomes magnetized when placed in a magnetic field. The movement of charge (normally **electrons***) also causes a magnetic field (see **electromagnetism**, pages 74-76).

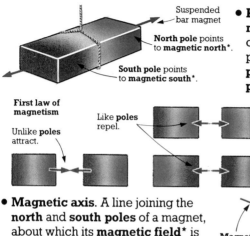

Suspended bar magnet

North pole points to **magnetic north***.

South pole points to **magnetic south***.

First law of magnetism

Unlike **poles** attract.

Like **poles** repel.

• **Pole.** A point in a magnet at which its **magnetic force*** appears to be concentrated. There are two types of pole – the **north** or **north seeking pole** and the **south** or **south seeking pole** (indentified by allowing the magnet to line up with the earth's **magnetic field***). All magnets have an equal number of each type of pole. The **first law of magnetism** states that unlike poles attract and like poles repel.

• **Magnetic axis.** A line joining the **north** and **south poles** of a magnet, about which its **magnetic field*** is symmetrical.

Magnetic axis

Magnetic axis

• **Ferromagnetic.** Describes a material which is strongly magnetic (i.e. is magnetized easily). Iron, nickel, cobalt and alloys of these are ferromagnetic, and are described as either **hard** or **soft**. **Sintered** materials (made by converting various mixtures of powders of the above metals into solids by heat and pressure) can be made magnetically very hard or soft by changing the metals used.

• **Hard.** Describes a **ferromagnetic** material which does not easily lose its magnetism after being magnetized, e.g. steel. Magnets made from these materials are called **permanent magnets**.

• **Soft.** Describes a **ferromagnetic** material which does not retain its magnetism after being magnetized, e.g. iron. Magnets made from these materials are called **temporary magnets**. **Residual magnetism** is the small amount of magnetism which can be left in magnetically soft materials.

Hard ferromagnetic materials are used as **permanent magnets**, e.g. as compass needles.

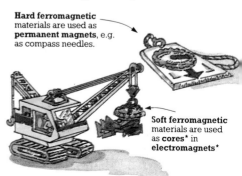

Soft ferromagnetic materials are used as **cores*** in **electromagnets***

Susceptibility. A measurement of the ability of a substance to become magnetized.
Ferromagnetic materials have a high susceptibility.

Unmagnetized magnetic material

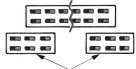

All **dipoles** aligned in a **domain**.

Overall effect of **domains** cancel each other out.

Magnetized

Domains ordered

When completely ordered (as here), magnet cannot become stronger – it is **saturated**.

Domain theory explains why magnets retain their **poles** when broken.

Two magnets formed, each with a **north** and **south** pole.

▲

Domain theory of magnetism. States that **ferromagnetic** materials consist of **dipoles** or **molecular magnets**, which interact with each other. These are all arranged in areas called **domains**, in which they all point in the same direction. A ferromagnetic material becomes magnetized when the domains become **ordered** (i.e. aligned).

Magnetization

When an object is magnetized, all the **dipoles** become aligned (see **domain theory**). This only happens when the object is in a **magnetic field*** and is called **induced magnetism**.

Induced magnetism

Magnetic material outside **magnetic field***

North end of **dipoles** attracted to **south pole** of magnet – object becomes magnetized.

Magnetic force* always attracts.

- **Single touch.** A method of magnetizing an object by stroking it repeatedly with the **pole** of a **permanent magnet** (see **hard**). Magnetism is induced in the object from the **magnetic field*** of the magnet.

Methods of magnetization (all involve **induced magnetism**)

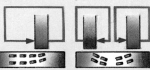

Single touch   Divided touch

Consequent poles are produced when like poles are used in **divided touch**.

- **Divided touch.** A method of magnetizing an object by stroking it repeatedly from the centre out with the opposite **poles** of two **permanent magnets** (see **hard**). Magnetism is induced in the object from the **magnetic field*** of the magnets.

- **Demagnetization.** The removal of magnetism from an object. This can be achieved by placing the object in a changing **magnetic field***, such as that created by a coil carrying **alternating current***. Alternatively, the **dipoles** (see **domain theory**) can be excited to point in random directions by hammering randomly or by heating above 700°C.

- **Self-demagnetization.** ▶ Loss of magnetism by a magnet because of the attraction of the **dipoles** (see **domain theory**) for the opposite **poles** of the magnet. It is reduced using pieces of soft iron (called **keepers**) arranged to form a closed loop of poles.

Self-demagnetization of bar magnet

Dipoles tend to turn.

Keepers for two bar magnets

Poles induced in keepers attract **dipoles**.

Magnetic fields

A **magnetic field** is a region around a **magnet** (see page 70) in which objects are affected by the **magnetic force***. The strength and direction of the magnetic field are shown by **magnetic field lines**.

- **Magnetic field lines** or **flux lines**. Lines which indicate the direction of the magnetic field around a magnet. They also show the strength of the field (see **magnetic flux density**). The direction of the field is the direction of the force on a **north pole***. Magnetic field lines are plotted by sprinkling iron filings around a magnet or by recording the direction of a **plotting compass** (a small compass with no directions marked on it) at various points.

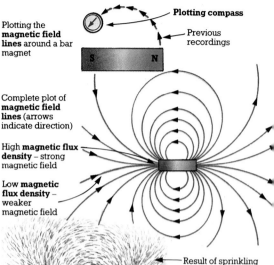

Plotting the **magnetic field lines** around a bar magnet

Complete plot of **magnetic field lines** (arrows indicate direction)

High **magnetic flux density** – strong magnetic field

Low **magnetic flux density** – weaker magnetic field

Plotting compass

Previous recordings

Result of sprinkling iron filings around magnet

Iron filings line up due to **induced magnetism***.

- **Magnetic flux density.** A measurement of the strength of a magnetic field at a point. This is shown by the closeness of the **magnetic field lines** to each other. Magnetic flux density is normally highest around the **poles***.

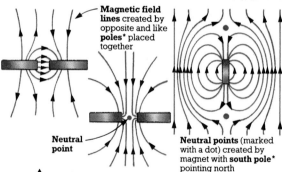

Magnetic field lines created by opposite and like **poles*** placed together

Neutral point

Neutral points (marked with a dot) created by magnet with **south pole*** pointing north

- **Neutral point.** A point of zero magnetism (the **magnetic flux density** is zero). It occurs where two or more magnetic fields interact with an equal but opposite effect. A bar magnet suspended along the **magnetic meridian**, with the **south pole*** pointing to the north, has two neutral points in line with its **magnetic axis***.

- **Diamagnetism.** Magnetism displayed by some substances when placed in a strong magnetic field. A piece of diamagnetic material tends to spread **magnetic field lines** out and lines up with its long side perpendicular to them. This effect is caused by **electrons*** being disturbed.

- **Paramagnetism.** Magnetism displayed by some substances when placed in a strong magnetic field. A piece of paramagnetic material tends to concentrate **magnetic field lines** through it and lines up with its long side parallel to them. It is caused by **dipoles*** moving slightly towards alignment.

* Dipole, 71; Electrons, 83; Induced magnetism, 71; Magnetic force, 6; Magnetic axis, Pole, 70.

The earth's magnetism

The earth has a magnetic field which acts as though there were a giant bar magnet in its centre, lined up approximately between its geographic north and south poles, although the angle is constantly changing. The **north pole*** of a compass points towards a point called **magnetic north**, its south pole to **magnetic south**.

Section through earth's magnetic field

Magnetic north

Magnetic field of earth acts as if imaginary magnet at centre with **south pole*** pointing to magnetic north.

Geographic north pole

Magnetic equator

- **Magnetic meridian**. The vertical plane containing the **magnetic axis*** of a magnet suspended in the earth's magnetic field (i.e. with its **north pole*** pointing to **magnetic north**).

- **Declination**. The angle between a line taken to true north (the geographic north pole) and one taken along the **magnetic meridian** (towards **magnetic north**) at a point. The position of magnetic north is gradually changing and so the declination alters slowly with time.

To geographic north or true north

Declination

To **magnetic north**

This plane is the **magnetic meridian**.

Direction of magnetic field

Freely suspended magnet

- **Isogonal lines**. Lines joining places with equal **declination**. These are redrawn from time to time because of the changing direction of the earth's magnetic field.

Horizontal line on earth's surface

- **Inclination** or **dip**. The angle between a horizontal line on the surface of the earth and the direction of the earth's magnetic field at a point. It is measured using a **dip circle** (see picture).

Inclination

Dip circle – magnet in **magnetic meridian** pivoted at centre to swing in vertical plane

- **Isoclinal line**. A line linking places with the same **inclination**.

- **Permeability**. A measure of the ability of a substance to "conduct" a magnetic field. Soft iron is much more permeable than air, so the magnetic field tends to be concentrated through it.

Soft iron has a higher **permeability** than air.

Magnetic field concentrated through iron

Magnetic field lines

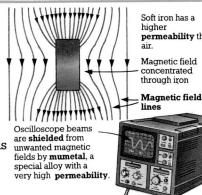

Oscilloscope beams are **shielded** from unwanted magnetic fields by **mumetal**, a special alloy with a very high **permeability**.

- **Shielding** or **screening**. The use of soft magnetic material to stop a magnetic field from reaching a point, effectively by "conducting" the field away. This is used in sensitive instruments, e.g. oscilloscopes.

* **Magnetic axis**, **Pole**, 70.

Electromagnetism

An electric current flowing through a wire produces a **magnetic field** (see pages 72-73) around the wire, the shape of which depends on the shape of the wire and the current flowing. These magnetic fields can be plotted in the same way as for **permanent magnets***. This effect, called **electromagnetism**, is used in very powerful magnets and also to produce motion from an electric current.

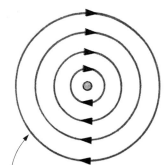

Cross-section of **magnetic field** due to wire carrying current directly into paper.

- **Ampere's swimming rule**. States that the north end of a compass needle placed near a current-carrying wire will be deflected towards the left hand of a person imagined to be swimming in the direction of the current and facing the wire.

Ampere's swimming rule

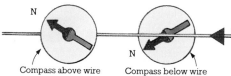

Compass above wire   Compass below wire

- **Maxwell's screw rule**. States that the direction of the magnetic field around a current-carrying wire is the way a screw turns when being screwed in the direction of the current.

Maxwell's screw rule

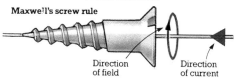

Direction of field   Direction of current

- **Right-hand grip rule**. States that the direction of a magnetic field around a wire is that from the base to the tips of the fingers if the wire is gripped by the right hand with the thumb pointing in the direction of the current.

Right hand grip rule

Direction of current

Direction of field

- **Coil**. A number of turns of current-carrying wire, produced by wrapping the wire around a shaped piece of material (a **former**). Examples are a **flat coil** and a **solenoid**.

- **Flat coil** or **plane coil**. A **coil** of wire whose length is small in comparison with its diameter.

- **Solenoid**. A **coil** whose length is large in comparison with its diameter. The magnetic field produced by a solenoid is similar to that produced by a bar magnet. The position of the **poles*** depends on the current direction (see diagram).

- **Core**. The material in the centre of a **coil** which dictates the strength of the field. Soft **ferromagnetic*** materials, most commonly soft iron, create the strongest magnetic field and are used in **electromagnets**.

Solenoid ▼

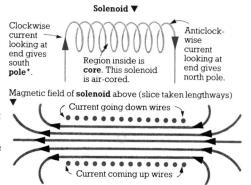

Clockwise current looking at end gives south **pole***.

Region inside is **core**. This solenoid is air-cored.

Anticlockwise current looking at end gives north pole.

Magnetic field of **solenoid** above (slice taken lengthways) ▼

Current going down wires

Current coming up wires

  * Ferromagnetic, 70; Permanent magnets, 70 (Hard); Pole, 70.

- **Electromagnet**. A **solenoid** with a **core** of soft strongly **ferromagnetic*** material. This forms a magnet which can be switched on and off simply by turning the current on and off. Practical electromagnets are constructed so that two opposite **poles*** are close to each other, producing a strong magnetic field. The electromagnet has a number of applications, some of which are shown below.

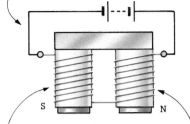
Electromagnet formed from two **solenoids** with iron **cores** and iron piece between ends.

Wire wound in opposite directions in each solenoid to produce opposite **poles***.

Applications of electromagnets

Electromagnets have a large number of applications, all of which use the fact that they attract metals when they are switched on and therefore convert **electric energy*** to **mechanical energy***. In two of the following examples, sound energy is produced from the mechanical energy.

- **Electric buzzer**. A device which ▶ produces a buzzing noise from **direct current***. A metal arm is attracted by an **electromagnet**, moves towards it, and in doing so breaks the circuit carrying current to the electromagnet. The arm is thus released and the process is repeated. The resulting vibration of the arm produces a buzzing noise. In the **electric bell**, a hammer attached to the arm repeatedly strikes a bell.

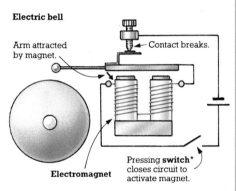
Electric bell

Arm attracted by magnet.

Contact breaks.

Electromagnet

Pressing **switch*** closes circuit to activate magnet.

- **Earpiece**. A device used to transform electrical signals to sound waves. The **permanent magnet*** attracts the metal diaphragm, but the strength of this attraction is changed as changing current (the incoming signals) flows through the coils of the **electromagnet**. The diaphragm thus vibrates to produce sound waves.

- **Relay**. A device in which a **switch*** is closed by the action of an **electromagnet**. A relatively small current in the **coil** of the electromagnet can be used to switch on a large current without the circuits being electrically linked.

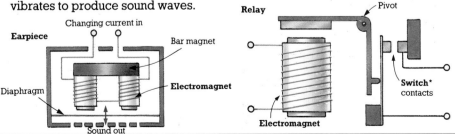

Earpiece

Changing current in

Bar magnet

Diaphragm

Electromagnet

Sound out

Relay

Pivot

Switch* contacts

Electromagnet

* **Direct current**, 60; **Electric energy**, 9; **Ferromagnetic**, 70; **Mechanical energy**, 9; **Permanent magnets**, 70 (**Hard**); **Pole**, 70; **Switch**, 64.

75

Electromagnets continued – the motor effect

The **motor effect** occurs when a current-carrying wire goes through a magnetic field. A force acts on the wire which can produce movement. This effect is used in **electric motors**, where **mechanical energy*** is produced from **electric energy***. The effect can also be used to measure current (see page 77), since the force depends on its magnitude.

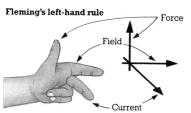
Fleming's left-hand rule

Force
Field
Current

- **Fleming's left-hand rule** or **motor ▶ rule**. The direction of the force on a wire carrying a current through a magnetic field can be worked out with the left hand (see diagram).

- **Electric motor**. A device which uses the **motor effect** to transform **electric energy*** to **mechanical energy***. The simplest motor consists of a current-carrying, square-shaped, flat **coil***, free to rotate in a magnetic field (see diagram). Motors produce a **back e.m.f.*** opposing the e.m.f. which drives them. This is produced because once the motor starts, it acts as a **generator*** (i.e. the movement of the coil in the field produces an opposing current).

- **Barlow's wheel**. A spiked, brass wheel in a magnetic field. Current enters at its centre and leaves from a spike which dips into mercury. The motor effect makes the wheel turn as the spikes dip into the mercury in turn.

- **Field windings**. Sets of **coils*** around the outside of an **electric motor**, which take the place of a permanent magnet to produce a stronger magnetic field. This increases the power of the motor.

- **Loudspeaker**. A device which uses the **motor effect** to transform electrical signals into **sound waves***. It consists of a **coil*** in a radial magnetic field (the direction of the field at any point is towards the centre). As the current changes, the coil, which is attached to a paper cone, moves in and out of the field (see diagram). The paper cone vibrates the air, producing sound waves which depend on the strength and frequency of the current.

Simple electric motor

Commutator. A ring split into two or more pieces, via which current enters and leaves the **coil*** of an **electric motor**. It ensures that the current enters the coil in the correct direction to make the motor rotate in one direction continuously.

Brushes. Contacts, normally made of carbon, through which current enters the **commutator** in an **electric motor**.

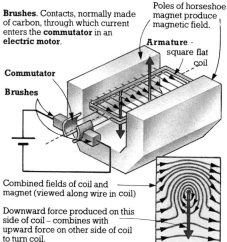

Poles of horseshoe magnet produce magnetic field.

Armature – square flat coil

Commutator

Brushes

Combined fields of coil and magnet (viewed along wire in coil)

Downward force produced on this side of coil – combines with upward force on other side of coil to turn coil.

Loudspeaker

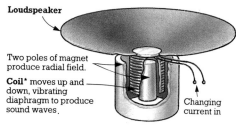

Two poles of magnet produce radial field.

Coil* moves up and down, vibrating diaphragm to produce sound waves.

Changing current in

* Back e.m.f., 60 (Electromotive force); Coil, 74; Electric energy, 9; Generator, 78; Mechanical energy, 9; Sound waves, 40.

Electric meters

Current can be detected by placing a suspended magnet near a wire and observing its deflection. This idea can be extended to produce a device (a **meter**) in which the deflection indicates on a scale the strength of the current. The current measuring device can then be adapted to measure **potential difference***.

- **Galvanometer.** Any device used to detect a **direct current*** by registering its magnetic effect. The simplest is a compass placed near a wire to simply show whether a current is present. The **moving coil galvanometer** uses the **motor effect** to show a deflection on a scale (see diagram).

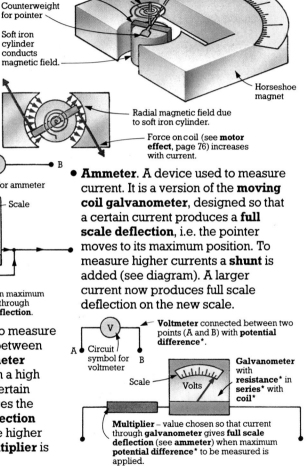

Moving coil galvanometer
Coil* of wire carries current
Counterweight for pointer
Soft iron cylinder conducts magnetic field.
Return spring
Pointer
Scale
Horseshoe magnet
Radial magnetic field due to soft iron cylinder.
Force on coil (see **motor effect**, page 76) increases with current.

Ammeter measures current flowing between A and B

A ●——(A)——● B

Circuit symbol for ammeter

Galvanometer
Scale
Amps
Current divides

Shunt – value chosen so that when maximum current to be read flows, current through galvanometer gives **full scale deflection**.

- **Ammeter.** A device used to measure current. It is a version of the **moving coil galvanometer**, designed so that a certain current produces a **full scale deflection**, i.e. the pointer moves to its maximum position. To measure higher currents a **shunt** is added (see diagram). A larger current now produces full scale deflection on the new scale.

- **Voltmeter.** A device used to measure the **potential difference*** between two points. It is a **galvanometer** between the two points with a high **resistance*** in **series***. A certain potential difference produces the current for a **full scale deflection** (see **ammeter**). To measure higher potential differences, a **multiplier** is added (see diagram).

A ●(V)

Circuit symbol for voltmeter

Voltmeter connected between two points (A and B) with **potential difference***.

Scale
Volts
Galvanometer with **resistance*** in **series*** with **coil***

Multiplier – value chosen so that current through **galvanometer** gives **full scale deflection** (see **ammeter**) when maximum **potential difference*** to be measured is applied.

- **Multimeter.** A **galvanometer** combined with the **shunts** (see **ammeter**) and **multipliers** (see **voltmeter**) necessary to measure currents and **potential differences***.

- **Moving iron meter.** A **meter** in which the current to be measured induces magnetism in two pieces of iron which attract or repel each other to produce a deflection.

* Coil, 74; **Direct current, 60**; **Potential difference**, 58; **Resistance**, 62; **Series**, 64.

77

Electromagnetic induction

Michael Faraday found that, as well as a current passing through a magnetic field producing movement (see **motor effect**, page 76), movement of a **conductor*** in a magnetic field produces an **electromotive force*** in the conductor. This effect, called **electromagnetic induction**, happens whenever a conductor is placed in a changing magnetic field.

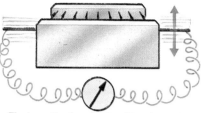

Electromotive force* induced by wire moving through magnetic field produces current, which then causes current through galvanometer*.

- **Faraday's law of induction**. States that the size of an induced electromotive force in a **conductor*** is proportional to the rate at which the magnetic field changes.

- **Lenz's law**. States that an induced electromotive force always acts to oppose the cause of it, e.g. in an **electric motor***, the e.m.f. produced because it acts as a **generator** opposes the e.m.f. driving the motor.

- **Fleming's right-hand rule** or **dynamo rule**. The direction of an induced current can be worked out from the direction of the magnetic field and the movement by using the right hand (see diagram).

Fleming's right-hand rule — Motion — Field — Current

- **Generator** or **dynamo**. A device used to produce electric current from **mechanical energy***. In the simplest generator (see diagram), an alternating electromotive force is induced in a **coil*** as it rotates in a magnetic field. A generator for **direct current*** has a **commutator***, as on an **electric motor***, which means the current always flows in the same direction.

- **Mutual induction**. The induction of an electromotive force in a **coil*** of wire by changing the current in a different coil. The changing current produces a changing magnetic field which induces a current in any other coil in the field. This was first demonstrated with **Faraday's iron ring**.

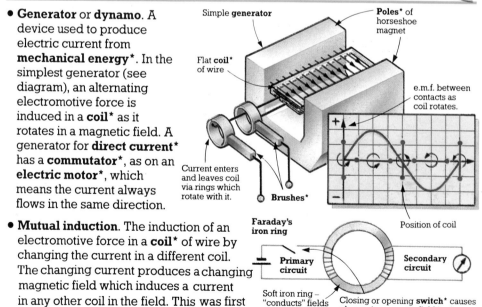

Simple **generator**

Flat **coil*** of wire

Poles* of horseshoe magnet

e.m.f. between contacts as coil rotates.

Current enters and leaves coil via rings which rotate with it.

Brushes*

Faraday's iron ring

Position of coil

Primary circuit

Secondary circuit

Soft iron ring – "conducts" fields between coils.

Closing or opening **switch*** causes change in magnetic field in ring which induces current in secondary circuit.

- **Self-induction.** The induction of an electromotive force in a **coil*** of wire due to the current inside it changing. For example, if the current in a coil is switched off, the resulting change in the magnetic field produces an electromotive force across the coil, in some cases much higher than that of the original.

- **Eddy current.** A current set up in a piece of metal when a magnetic field around it changes, even though the metal may not be part of a circuit. Eddy currents can cause unwanted heat energy, e.g. in the iron core of a **transformer.**

Transformers

A **transformer** consists of two **coils*** of wire wound onto the same **core*** of soft **ferromagnetic*** material. It is used to change an alternating electromotive force in one of the coils to a different e.m.f. in the other coil, e.g. in electricity supply, see page 61. Hardly any energy is lost between the two circuits in a well designed transformer.

- **Turns ratio.** The ratio of the number of turns in the **primary coil** in a **transformer** to the number of turns in the **secondary coil.** The turns ratio is also the ratio of the electromotive force in the primary coil to the electromotive force in the secondary coil.

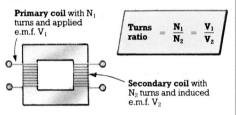

Primary coil with N_1 turns and applied e.m.f. V_1

$$\text{Turns ratio} = \frac{N_1}{N_2} = \frac{V_1}{V_2}$$

Secondary coil with N_2 turns and induced e.m.f. V_2

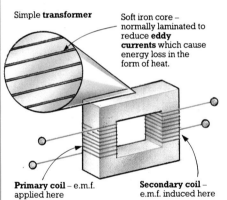

Simple **transformer**

Soft iron core – normally laminated to reduce **eddy currents** which cause energy loss in the form of heat.

Primary coil – e.m.f. applied here

Secondary coil – e.m.f. induced here

- **Primary coil.** The **coil*** in a **transformer** to which an alternating electromotive force is applied in order to produce an electromotive force in the **secondary coil.**

- **Secondary coil.** The **coil*** in a **transformer** in which an alternating electromotive force is induced by the electromotive force applied to the **primary coil.** Some transformers have two or more secondary coils.

- **Step-up transformer.** A **transformer** in which the electromotive force in the **secondary coil** is greater than that in the **primary coil.** The **turns ratio** is less than one.

Step-up transformer

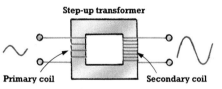

Primary coil   Secondary coil

- **Step-down transformer.** A **transformer** in which the electromotive force in the **secondary coil** is less than that in the **primary coil.** The **turns ratio** is greater than one.

Step-down transformer

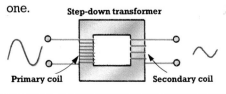

Primary coil   Secondary coil

* **Coil, Core,** 74; **Ferromagnetic,** 70.

Cathode rays

A **cathode ray** is a continual stream of **electrons** (negatively-charged particles – see page 83) travelling through a low pressure gas or a vacuum. It is produced when electrons are freed from a metal **cathode***, and attracted to an **anode***. Cathode rays have a number of applications, from the production of **X-rays*** to **television**, all of which involve the use of a shaped glass tube (called an **electron tube**) containing a low pressure gas or a vacuum for the rays to travel in. The rays are normally produced by an **electron gun**, which forms part of the tube.

● **Electron gun**. A device which produces a continuous stream of electrons (a cathode ray). It consists of a heated **cathode*** which gives off electrons (this is called **thermionic emission**) and an **anode*** which attracts them to form a stream.

● **Maltese cross tube**. An **electron tube** in which the cathode ray is interrupted by a cross which casts a "shadow" on a **fluorescent*** screen at the end of the tube. This shows the electrons are moving in straight lines.

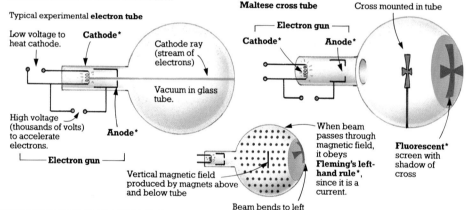

● **Discharge tube**. A gas-filled glass tube in which **ions*** and electrons are attracted by the **electrodes*** and move towards them at high speed. As they do so, they collide with gas atoms, causing these atoms to split into more ions and electrons, and emit

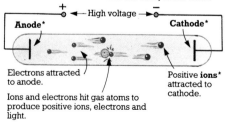

+ ◀— High voltage —▶ ─
Anode*   **Cathode***

Electrons attracted to anode.

Positive **ions*** attracted to cathode.

Ions and electrons hit gas atoms to produce positive ions, electrons and light.

light at the same time. The colour of the light depends on the gas used, e.g. neon produces orange light (used in advertising displays) and mercury vapour produces blue-green light (used for street lighting). Discharge tubes use up to five times less electricity than other lighting. A **fluorescent tube** is a discharge tube filled with mercury vapour, which emits **ultraviolet radiation***. This hits the inside of the tube, causing its coating of special powder to give out **visible light*** (see **fluorescence**, page 45).

* **Anode, Cathode**, 66 (**Electrode**); **Fleming's left-hand rule** 76; **Fluorescence**, 45; **Ions**, 88 (**Ionization**); **Ultraviolet radiation**, 44; **Visible light**, 45; **X-rays**, 44.

X-ray tube. A special electron tube used to produce a beam of **X-rays***. A cathode ray hits a tungsten target which stops the electrons suddenly. This causes X-rays to be emitted.

High voltage
Low voltage to heat cathode
Vacuum in glass tube
Anode*
X-rays*
produced
Cathode*

The cathode ray oscilloscope

The **cathode ray oscilloscope (CRO)** is an instrument used to study currents and **potential differences***. A cathode ray from an **electron gun** produces a spot on a **fluorescent*** screen. In normal use, the ray is repeatedly swept across the back of the screen at a selected speed and so produces a visible trace across the front. If a signal is fed into the oscilloscope, the vertical position of the beam will change according to the strength of the signal and the trace on the screen then shows this change over time.

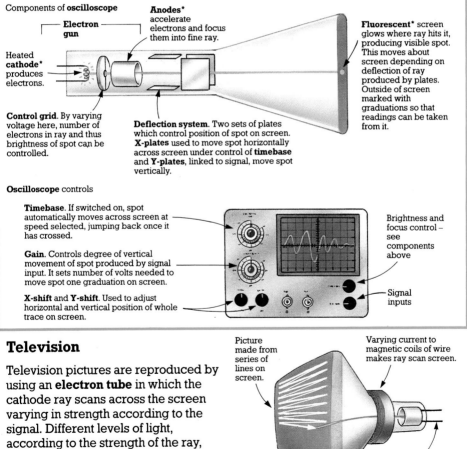

Components of **oscilloscope**

Electron gun

Anodes* accelerate electrons and focus them into fine ray.

Heated **cathode*** produces electrons.

Fluorescent* screen glows where ray hits it, producing visible spot. This moves about screen depending on deflection of ray produced by plates. Outside of screen marked with graduations so that readings can be taken from it.

Control grid. By varying voltage here, number of electrons in ray and thus brightness of spot can be controlled.

Deflection system. Two sets of plates which control position of spot on screen. **X-plates** used to move spot horizontally across screen under control of **timebase** and **Y-plates**, linked to signal, move spot vertically.

Oscilloscope controls

Timebase. If switched on, spot automatically moves across screen at speed selected, jumping back once it has crossed.

Gain. Controls degree of vertical movement of spot produced by signal input. It sets number of volts needed to move spot one graduation on screen.

X-shift and **Y-shift**. Used to adjust horizontal and vertical position of whole trace on screen.

Brightness and focus control – see components above

Signal inputs

Television

Television pictures are reproduced by using an **electron tube** in which the cathode ray scans across the screen varying in strength according to the signal. Different levels of light, according to the strength of the ray, are given off from different parts of the screen to produce a picture.

Picture made from series of lines on screen.

Varying current to magnetic coils of wire makes ray scan screen.

Signal varies strength of ray from **electron gun**.

* **Anode, Cathode**, 66 (**Electrode**); **Fluorescence**, 45; **Potential difference**, 58; **X-rays**, 44.

Atomic structure

A great deal has been learnt about the physical nature of atoms (see also page 4) since Greek philosophers first proposed that all matter was made of basic indivisible "building blocks". It is now known that an atom is not indivisible, but has a complex internal structure, consisting of many different smaller particles (**subatomic particles**) and a lot of empty space.

- **Rutherford-Bohr atom.** A "solar system" representation of an atom, devised by Ernest Rutherford and Niels Bohr in 1911. It is now known to be incorrect (**electrons** have no regular "orbits" – see **electron shells**).

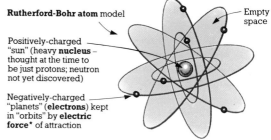

Rutherford-Bohr atom model

Empty space

Positively-charged "sun" (heavy **nucleus** – thought at the time to be just protons; neutron not yet discovered)

Negatively-charged "planets" (**electrons**) kept in "orbits" by **electric force*** of attraction

- **Nucleus** (pl. **nuclei**) or **atomic nucleus**. The central core of an atom, consisting of closely-packed **nucleons** (**protons** and **neutrons**).

Nucleus – (almost all the mass of the atom, but very tiny – its radius is approx. 1/10000th that of the atom)

Proton (mass approx. 1836 times that of an electron)

Neutron (mass approx. 1840 times that of an electron)

- **Protons.** Positively-charged particles in the **nucleus**. The number of protons (**atomic number**) identifies the element and equals the number of **electrons**, so atoms are electrically neutral.

- **Neutrons.** Electrically neutral particles in the **nucleus**. The number of neutrons in atoms of the same element can vary (see **isotope**).

- **Mass number (A).** The number of **protons** and **neutrons** (**nucleons**) in a **nucleus**. It is the whole number nearest to the **relative atomic mass** of the atom, and is important in identifying **isotopes**.

- **Atomic number (Z).** The number of **protons** in a **nucleus** (hence also the number of **electrons** around it). All atoms with the same atomic number are of the same element (see also **isotope**).

- **Neutron number (N).** The number of **neutrons** in a **nucleus**. See also graph, page 87.

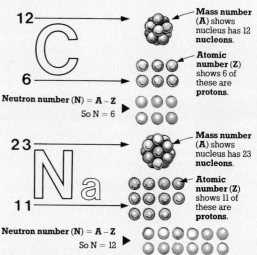

The **mass** and **atomic numbers** are often written with the symbol of an element:

12 C **6**

Mass number (**A**) shows nucleus has 12 nucleons.

Atomic number (**Z**) shows 6 of these are protons.

Neutron number (**N**) = **A** – **Z**
So N = 6

23 Na **11**

Mass number (**A**) shows nucleus has 23 nucleons.

Atomic number (**Z**) shows 11 of these are protons.

Neutron number (**N**) = **A** – **Z**
So N = 12

Electrons. Particles with a negative charge and very small mass. They move around the **nucleus** in **electron shells**. See also **proton**.

Electron shells. Regions of space around a **nucleus** containing moving **electrons**. An atom can have up to seven (from the inside, called the **K, L, M, N, O, P** and **Q shells**). Each can hold up to a certain number of electrons (the first four, from the inside, can take up to 2, 8, 18 and 32 electrons respectively). The further away the shell is from the nucleus, the higher the energy of its electrons (the shell has a given **energy level**). The **outer shell** is the last shell with electrons in it. If this is full or has an **octet** (8 electrons), the atom is very stable (see page 84).

The positions of electrons in their shells cannot be exactly determined at any one time, but each shell consists of **orbitals**, or **probability clouds**. Each of these is a region in which one or two electrons are likely to be found at any time.

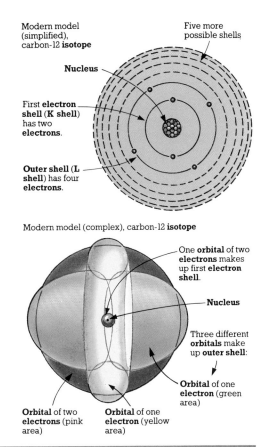

Modern model (simplified), carbon-12 **isotope**

Five more possible shells

Nucleus

First **electron shell (K shell)** has two **electrons**.

Outer shell (L shell) has four **electrons**.

Modern model (complex), carbon-12 **isotope**

One **orbital** of two **electrons** makes up first **electron shell**.

Nucleus

Three different **orbitals** make up **outer shell**:

Orbital of one **electron** (green area)

Orbital of two **electrons** (pink area)

Orbital of one **electron** (yellow area)

Isotopes. Different forms of the same element, with the same atomic number, but different **neutron numbers** and hence different **mass numbers**. There are isotopes of every element, since even if only one natural form exists (i.e. the element is **monoisotopic**), others can be made artificially (see **radioisotope**, page 86).

Mass numbers are used with names or symbols when isotopes are being specified:

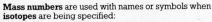

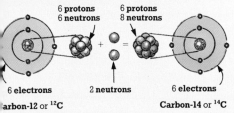

6 **protons**
6 **neutrons**

6 **protons**
8 **neutrons**

6 **electrons**

2 **neutrons**

6 **electrons**

Carbon-12 or ^{12}C

Carbon-14 or ^{14}C

● **Relative atomic mass**. Also called **atomic mass** or **atomic weight**. The mass of an atom in **unified atomic mass units (u)**. Each of these is equal to $\frac{1}{12}$ of the mass of a carbon-12 atom (**isotope**). The relative atomic mass of a carbon-12 atom is thus 12 u, but no other values are whole numbers, e.g. 26.9815 u (aluminium).

The relative atomic mass takes into account the various isotopes of the element, if these occur in a natural sample. Natural chlorine, for example, has three chlorine-35 atoms to every one of chlorine-37, and the relative atomic mass of chlorine (35.453 u) is a proportional average of the two different masses of these isotopes.

Atomic and nuclear energy

All things, whether large objects or minute particles, have a particular **energy state**, or level of **potential energy*** ("stored" energy). Moreover, they will always try to find their lowest possible energy state, called the **ground state**, which is the state of the greatest stability. In most cases, this involves recombining in some way, i.e. adding or losing constituents, and in all cases it results in the release of the "excess" energy – in large amounts if the particles are atoms, and vast amounts if they are nuclei. The greater the **binding energy** of an atom or nucleus, the greater its stability, i.e. the less likely it is to undergo any change.

• **Binding energy (B.E.).** The energy input needed to split a given atom or nucleus into its constituent parts (see pages 82-83). The **potential energy*** of an atom or nucleus is less than the total potential energy of its parts when these are apart. This is because, when they came together, the parts found a lower (collective) **energy state** (see introduction and **nuclear force**), and so lost energy. The binding energy is a measure of this difference in potential energy – it is the energy needed to "go back the other way" – so the greater it is, the lower the potential energy of an atom or nucleus and the greater its stability. Binding energy varies from atom to atom and nucleus to nucleus.

• **Nuclear force.** The strong force which keeps the parts of a nucleus (**nucleons***) together and overcomes the **electric force*** of repulsion between the **protons***. Its effect varies according to the size of the nucleus (see graph) as the force

• **Mass defect.** The mass of an atom or nucleus is less than the sum of the masses of its parts when these are apart. The difference is the mass defect. It is the mass of the **potential energy*** lost when the parts came together (see **binding energy** and formula below).

Einstein showed that energy has mass. Hence any loss of **potential energy*** also results in a loss of mass – the mass of the energy itself.
Einstein's mass-energy formula:

$$E = mc^2$$

where E = energy in joules; m = mass in kilograms; $c = 3 \times 10^8$ (numerical value of speed of light in m s^{-1}).

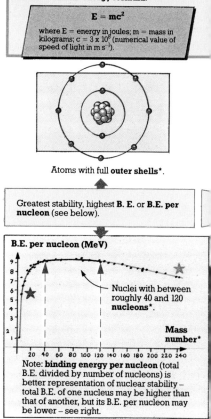

Atoms with full **outer shells***.

Greatest stability, highest **B. E.** or **B.E. per nucleon** (see below).

B.E. per nucleon (MeV)

Nuclei with between roughly 40 and 120 **nucleons***.

Mass number*

Note: **binding energy per nucleon** (total B.E. divided by number of nucleons) is better representation of nuclear stability – total B.E. of one nucleus may be higher than that of another, but its B.E. per nucleon may be lower – see right.

only acts between immediately neighbouring nucleons. The greater the attractive effect of the nuclear force, the higher the **binding energy** of the nucleus (i.e. the more energy was lost when the parts came together).

* Electric force, 6; Mass number, 82; Nucleons, 82 (Nucleus); Outer shell, 83 (Electron shells); Potential energy, 8; Protons, 82.

- **Quantum theory**. States that energy takes the form of minute, separate "chunks" called **quanta** (sing. **quantum**), rather than a steady stream. The theory was originally limited to energy emitted by bodies (i.e. **electromagnetic wave*** energy), though all other kinds of energy (see pages 8-9) are now generally included. Electromagnetic quanta are now specified as **photons**. The theory further states that the amount of energy carried by a photon is proportional to the **frequency*** of the emitted electromagnetic radiation (see pages 44-45).

Energy carried by **quantum (photon)**:

$$E = hf$$

where E = energy in joules; h = **Planck's constant** $(6.63 \times 10^{-34}\ J\ s^{-1})$; f = **frequency*** in Hertz.

Electron volt (eV). Unit of atomic energy, equal to energy gained by one electron moved through **potential difference*** of 1 V.

$$1\ eV = 1.6 \times 10^{-19}\ J$$

Megaelectron volt (MeV). Unit of nuclear energy, equal to 1 million eV.

$$1\ MeV = 1.6 \times 10^{-13}\ J$$

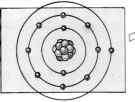

Few **electrons*** in outer shell, or nearly a full outer shell, i.e. just one or two electrons missing.

Putting unstable atoms together with other unstable atoms causes them to react – electrons transferred, i.e. recombinations take place.

Change in energy state of atom or nucleus is atomic or nuclear **transition**. Change resulting in change in chemical properties (i.e. different element) is **transformation** or **transmutation**.

Less stable, low B.E. or B.E. per nucleon.

Result always release of energy ("excess" energy). Particles gain greater stability – total overall B.E. or B.E. per nucleon higher than before. Energy released as heat and **kinetic energy*** of particles.

As shown, finding higher B.E. (lower energy state) may occur with very little "help", e.g. putting unstable atoms together or in the case of spontaneous radioactivity. In other cases, energy may need to be added (heating atoms, nuclei or particles).

Few **nucleons*** and hence relatively large surface area. Only a few nucleons (relative to whole number) have "pulling" **nuclear force** acting on them from neighbours on all sides, so overall effect of nuclear force is less.

Or

Heating nuclei gives them high **kinetic energy*** and means two will join when they collide (see **fusion**, page 93).

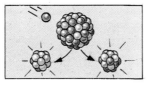

Hitting nucleus with fast particle causes it to split (see **fission**, page 92).

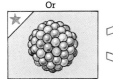

Very large number of nucleons. Means more **protons*** – **electric force*** of repulsion has more effect, overall effect of nuclear force is less.

Some heavy nuclei release particles spontaneously (see **radioactivity**, page 86).

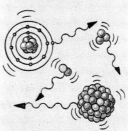

If not enough energy added, energy re-released as **photons** (see **quantum theory**). In atoms, electrons "fall" back and type (**frequency***) of photons emitted depends on shells between which they move. **X-rays*** (highest frequency, most energy) if innermost shells, **UV radiation*** if shells further out, and so on (see spectrum, page 44). With nuclei, always γ-**rays*** (more energy involved).

---

* Electric force, 6; Electromagnetic waves, 44; Electrons, 83; Frequency, 16, 35; Kinetic energy, 9; Nucleons, 82 (**Nucleus**); Potential difference, 58; Protons, 82; Ultra-violet (**UV**) radiation, X-rays, 44; Gamma (γ) rays, 44, 86.

Radioactivity

Radioactivity is a property of some unstable **nuclei** (see pages 82 and 84), whereby they break up spontaneously into nuclei of other elements and emit **radiation***, a process known as **radioactive decay**.

There are three types of radiation emitted by radioactive elements – streams of **alpha particles** (called **alpha rays**), streams of **beta particles** (**beta rays**) and **gamma rays**. For more about the detection and uses of radiation, see pages 88-91.

• **Radioisotope** or **radioactive isotope**. Any radioactive substance (all substances are effectively **isotopes** – see page 83). There are several naturally-occurring radioisotopes, most of which still exist because they have very long **half-lives** (e.g. uranium-238), though one, carbon-14, is continually produced by **cosmic rays** (see **background radiation**, page 88). Other radioisotopes are produced by **nuclear fission***, and more still are produced in research centres, where nuclei are hit by fast particles (ranging from **protons*** to

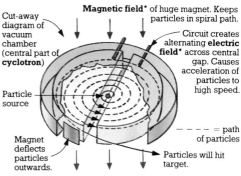

Cut-away diagram of vacuum chamber (central part of **cyclotron**)

Particle source

Magnet deflects particles outwards.

Magnetic field* of huge magnet. Keeps particles in spiral path.

Circuit creates alternating **electric field*** across central gap. Causes acceleration of particles to high speed.

– – – – = path of particles

Particles will hit target.

uranium nuclei, most often **neutrons***). These are speeded up in **particle accelerators**, e.g. **cyclotrons** (see above).

• **Alpha particles** (**α-particles**). Positively-charged particles ejected from some radioactive nuclei (see **alpha decay**). They are relatively heavy (two **protons*** and two **neutrons***), move relatively slowly and have a low penetrating power.

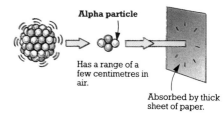

Alpha particle

Has a range of a few centimetres in air.

Absorbed by thick sheet of paper.

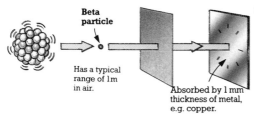

Beta particle

Has a typical range of 1m in air.

Absorbed by 1 mm thickness of metal, e.g. copper.

• **Beta particles** (**β-particles**). Particles ejected from some radioactive nuclei at about the speed of light. There are two types – **electrons*** and **positrons**, which have the same mass as electrons, but a positive charge. See **beta decay**.

• **Gamma rays** (**γ-rays**). Invisible **electromagnetic waves** (see also page 44). They have the highest penetrating power and are generally, though not always, emitted from a radioactive nucleus after an **alpha** or **beta particle**.

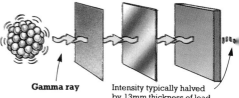

Gamma ray

Intensity typically halved by 13mm thickness of lead (or 120m of air).

* Electric field, 58; Electrons, 83; Magnetic field, 72; Neutrons, 82; Nuclear fission, 92; Protons, 82; Radiation, 9.

- **Radioactive decay.** The spontaneous splitting up of a radioactive nucleus, which results in the ejection of **alpha** or **beta particles**, often followed by **gamma rays**. When a nucleus ejects such a particle, i.e. undergoes a nuclear **disintegration**, energy is released (see page 84), and a different nucleus (and atom) is formed. If this is also radioactive, the decay process continues until a stable (non-radioactive) atom is reached. Such a series of disintegrations is called a **decay series, decay chain,** **radioactive series** or **transformation series.**

- **Half-life ($T^{1}/_{2}$).** The time it takes for half the atoms in a sample to undergo **radioactive decay**, and hence for the radiation emitted to be halved. This is all that can be accurately predicted – it is impossible to predict the decay of any single atom, since they decay individually and randomly. The range of half-lives is vast, e.g. strontium-90, 28 years; uranium-238, 4.5×10^9 years.

The rate of **radioactive decay** is measured in **becquerels (Bq)**. One becquerel equals one **disintegration** per second. An older unit, the **curie**, equals 3.7×10^{10} becquerels.

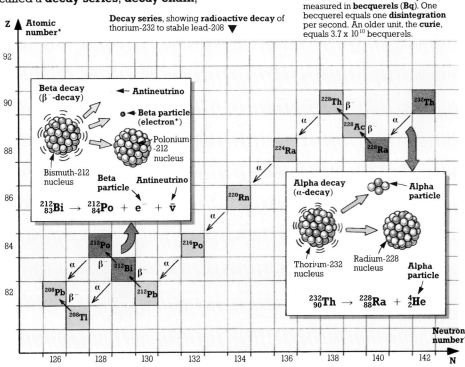

Decay series, showing **radioactive decay** of thorium-232 to stable lead-208 ▼

Alpha decay (α-decay). The loss of an **alpha particle** by a radioactive nucleus. This decreases the **atomic number*** by two and the **mass number*** by four, and so a new nucleus is formed.

- **Beta decay (β-decay).** The loss of either kind of **beta particle** by a radioactive nucleus. The electron (β^- or e^-) is ejected (with another particle called an **antineutrino**) when a **neutron*** decays into a **proton***. The positron (β^+ or e^+) is ejected (with another particle called a **neutrino**) when a proton decays into a neutron. Beta decay thus increases or decreases the **atomic number*** by one (the **mass number*** stays the same).

---

* **Atomic number**, 82; **Electrons**, 83; **Mass number, Neutron number, Neutrons, Protons**, 82.

Detecting and measuring radioactivity

Radioactive substances (**radioisotopes***) have special hazard warning labels.

Radioactive source for laboratory use

Drums of radioactive waste

There are a number of devices which detect and measure the radiation emitted by radioactive substances (**radioisotopes***). Some are used mainly in laboratories (to study artificially produced radioisotopes); others have a wider range of uses (e.g. as monitoring devices for safety purposes) and can also be used to detect **background radiation**. Most of the devices detect and measure the radiation by monitoring the **ionization** it causes – see **Geiger counter** and **pulse electroscope**, right, and **cloud** and **bubble chambers**, page 90.

- **Background radiation**. Radiation present on earth (in relatively small amounts), originating both from natural and unnatural sources. One notable natural source is carbon-14, which is taken in by plants and animals. This is constantly being produced from stable nitrogen-14 due to bombardment by **cosmic rays** (**cosmic radiation**) entering the atmosphere from outer space. These are streams of particles of enormously high energy. The **background count** is a measure of the background radiation.

- **Ionization**. The creation of **ions** (electrically-charged particles), which occurs when atoms (electrically neutral) lose or gain **electrons***, creating **cations** (positive ions) or **anions** (negative ions)

Ionization

Atom loses **electron***.   Atom gains electron.

Cation formed (more **protons*** than electrons).

Anion formed (more electrons than protons).

Ionization due to radiation

Atom

Particle glances off atom.

Cation formed

Radiation particle   Electrons "knocked out" to become free electrons.

Natural sources, e.g. rocks, plants and animals

Unnatural sources, e.g. industry, medicine, weapons testing

Measuring the background count with a **Geiger counter**.

respectively. In the case of radiation, **alpha** and **beta particles*** ionize the atoms of substances they pass through, usually creating cations. This is because their energy is so high that they cause one or more electrons to be "knocked out" of the atoms. **Gamma rays*** can also ionize atoms.

 * Alpha particles, Beta particles, 86; Electrons, 83; Gamma rays, 86; Protons, 82; Radioisotope, 86.

Detection devices

Geiger counter. A piece of apparatus consisting of a **Geiger-Müller tube**, a **scaler** and/or **ratemeter** and often a loudspeaker. The tube is a gas-filled cylinder with two **electrodes*** – its walls act as the **cathode***, and it has a central wire **anode***. The whole apparatus indicates the presence of radiation by registering pulses of current between the electrodes. These pulses result from the **ionization** the radiation causes in the gas (normally low pressure argon, plus a trace of bromine). A scaler is an electronic counter which counts the pulses and a ratemeter measures the count rate – the average rate of pulses in counts per second.

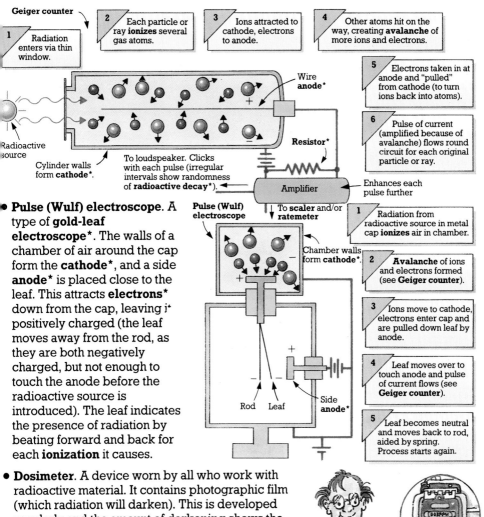

Geiger counter

1 Radiation enters via thin window.

2 Each particle or ray **ionizes** several gas atoms.

3 Ions attracted to cathode, electrons to anode.

4 Other atoms hit on the way, creating **avalanche** of more ions and electrons.

Wire **anode***

Radioactive source

Cylinder walls form **cathode***.

To loudspeaker. Clicks with each pulse (irregular intervals show randomness of **radioactive decay***).

Resistor*

Amplifier

Enhances each pulse further

5 Electrons taken in at anode and "pulled" from cathode (to turn ions back into atoms).

6 Pulse of current (amplified because of avalanche) flows round circuit for each original particle or ray.

Pulse (Wulf) electroscope. A type of **gold-leaf electroscope***. The walls of a chamber of air around the cap form the **cathode***, and a side **anode*** is placed close to the leaf. This attracts **electrons*** down from the cap, leaving i* positively charged (the leaf moves away from the rod, as they are both negatively charged, but not enough to touch the anode before the radioactive source is introduced). The leaf indicates the presence of radiation by beating forward and back for each **ionization** it causes.

Pulse (Wulf) electroscope

To **scaler** and/or **ratemeter**

Chamber walls form **cathode***.

Rod   Leaf   Side **anode***

1 Radiation from radioactive source in metal cap **ionizes** air in chamber.

2 **Avalanche** of ions and electrons formed (see **Geiger counter**).

3 Ions move to cathode, electrons enter cap and are pulled down leaf by anode.

4 Leaf moves over to touch anode and pulse of current flows (see **Geiger counter**).

5 Leaf becomes neutral and moves back to rod, aided by spring. Process starts again.

Dosimeter. A device worn by all who work with radioactive material. It contains photographic film (which radiation will darken). This is developed regularly and the amount of darkening shows the **dose** of radiation the wearer has been exposed to.

Dosimeter

* **Anode, Cathode, Electrode,** 66; **Electrons,** 83; **Gold-leaf electroscope,** 56 (**Electroscope**); **Radioactive decay,** 87; **Resistor,** 62.

Detection devices (continued)

- **Cloud chamber**. A device in which the paths taken by **alpha** and **beta** particles* show up as tracks. This happens when the vapour in the chamber (alcohol or water vapour) is turned into **supersaturated** vapour by cooling (in one of two different ways – see below). This is vapour below the temperature at which it should condense, but which does not condense because there are no dust or other particles for droplets to form around.

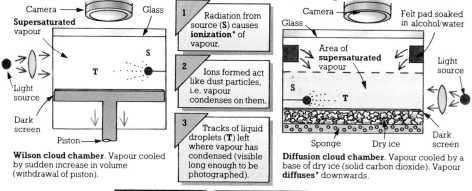

Camera → Glass
Supersaturated vapour
S
T
Light source
Dark screen
Piston

Wilson cloud chamber. Vapour cooled by sudden increase in volume (withdrawal of piston).

1 Radiation from source (**S**) causes **ionization*** of vapour.

2 Ions formed act like dust particles, i.e. vapour condenses on them.

3 Tracks of liquid droplets (**T**) left where vapour has condensed (visible long enough to be photographed).

Camera → Glass
Area of **supersaturated** vapour
S
T
Felt pad soaked in alcohol/water
Light source
Sponge   Dry ice
Dark screen

Diffusion cloud chamber. Vapour cooled by a base of dry ice (solid carbon dioxide). Vapour **diffuses*** downwards.

Cloud chamber tracks (produced at irregular intervals, showing random nature of **radioactive decay***).

Tracks made by heavy α-**particles*** are short, straight and thick.

Tracks made by light β-**particles*** are long, straggly and thin.

Gamma rays* do not create tracks themselves, but can knock **electrons*** out of single atoms. These then speed away and create tracks like β-particle tracks (see left).

- **Bubble chamber**. A device which, like a cloud chamber, shows particle tracks. It contains **superheated** liquid (usually hydrogen or helium) – liquid heated to above its boiling point, but not actually boiling because it is under pressure. After the pressure is suddenly lowered, nuclear particles entering the chamber cause **ionization*** of the liquid atoms. Wherever this occurs, the energy released makes the liquid boil, producing tracks of bubbles.

Bubble chamber tracks. Generally curved, because magnetic field set up to deflect particles (leads to better identification).

- **Scintillation counter**. A device which detects **gamma rays***. It consists of a **scintillation crystal** and a **photomultiplier** tube. The crystal is made of a **phosphor*** (e.g. sodium iodide). Phosphors emit light flashes (**scintillations**) when hit by radiation.

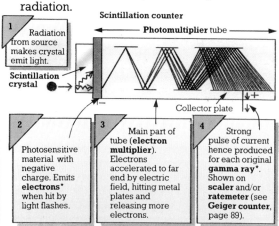

Scintillation counter

Photomultiplier tube

1 Radiation from source makes crystal emit light.

Scintillation crystal

Collector plate

2 Photosensitive material with negative charge. Emits **electrons*** when hit by light flashes.

3 Main part of tube (**electron multiplier**). Electrons accelerated to far end by electric field, hitting metal plates and releasing more electrons.

4 Strong pulse of current hence produced for each original **gamma ray***. Shown on **scaler** and/or **ratemeter** (see **Geiger counter**, page 89).

* Alpha particles, Beta particles, 86; Diffusion, 5; Electrons, 83; Gamma rays, 86; Ionization, 88; Phosphor, 45 (Phosphorescence); Radioactive decay, 87.

Uses of radioactivity

The radiation emitted by **radioisotopes*** (radioactive substances) can be put to a variety of uses, particularly in the fields of medicine, industry and archaeological research.

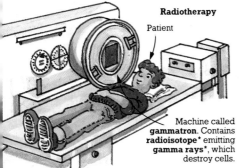

Radiotherapy

Patient

Machine called **gammatron**. Contains **radioisotope*** emitting **gamma rays***, which destroy cells.

- **Radiology**. The study of radioactivity and **X-rays***, especially with regard to their use in medicine.

- **Radiotherapy**. The use of the radiation emitted by **radioisotopes*** to treat disease. All living cells are susceptible to radiation, so it is possible to destroy malignant (cancer) cells by using carefully controlled doses of radiation.

- **Radioactive tracing**. A method of following the ▶ path of a substance through an object, and detecting its concentration as it moves. This is done by introducing a **radioisotope*** into the substance and tracking the radiation it emits. The radioisotope used is called a **tracer**, and the substance is said to be **labelled**. In medical diagnosis, for example, high levels of the radioisotope in an organ may indicate the presence of malignant (cancer) cells. The radioisotopes used always have short **half-lives*** and decay into harmless substances.

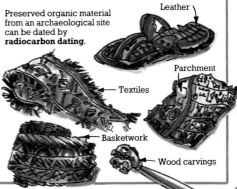

Patient has swallowed **labelled** substance.

Scanner (**gamma camera**) picks up **radioisotope*** in body.

Sample **scan** (doctor can locate diseased areas from different colours).

Testing for faults in the welding of a metal pipe.

Machine containing **radioisotope*** takes **radiograph**.

◀ • **Gamma radiography** (γ-**radiography**). The production of a **radiograph** (similar to a photograph) by the use of **gamma rays*** (see also **X-radiography**, page 44). This has many uses, including quality control in industry.

- **Radiocarbon dating** or **carbon dating**. A way of calculating the time elapsed since living matter died. All living things contain a small amount of carbon-14 (a **radioisotope*** absorbed from the atmosphere), which continues to emit radiation after death. This emission gradually decreases (carbon-14 has a **half-life*** of 5,700 years), so the age of the remains can be calculated from its strength.

Preserved organic material from an archaeological site can be dated by **radiocarbon dating**.

Leather

Parchment

Textiles

Basketwork

Wood carvings

* **Gamma rays**, 86; **Half-life**, 87; **Radioisotope**, 86; **X-rays**, 44.

91

Nuclear fission and fusion

The central **nucleus** of an atom (see page 82) holds vast amounts of "stored" energy (see pages 84-85). **Nuclear fission** and **nuclear fusion** are both ways in which this energy can be released. They are both **nuclear reactions** (reactions which bring about a change in the nucleus).

• **Nuclear fission.** The process in which a heavy, unstable nucleus splits up into two (or more) lighter nuclei, roughly equal in size, with the release of two or three **neutrons*** (**fission neutrons**) and a large amount of energy (see also page 84). The two lighter nuclei are called **fission products** or **fission fragments** and many of them are **radioactive***. Fission is made to happen (see **induced fission**) in **fission reactors*** to produce heat energy. It does not often occur naturally (**spontaneous fission**).

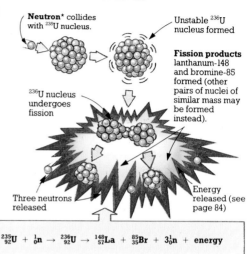

Induced fission of uranium-235

Neutron* collides with ^{235}U nucleus.

Unstable ^{236}U nucleus formed

^{236}U nucleus undergoes fission

Fission products lanthanum-148 and bromine-85 formed (other pairs of nuclei of similar mass may be formed instead).

Three neutrons released

Energy released (see page 84)

Nuclear equation for reaction, above right (see **mass** and **atomic numbers**, page 82):

$$^{235}_{92}U + {}^{1}_{0}n \rightarrow {}^{236}_{92}U \rightarrow {}^{148}_{57}La + {}^{85}_{35}Br + 3{}^{1}_{0}n + energy$$

• **Spontaneous fission. Nuclear fission** which occurs naturally, i.e. without assistance from an outside agency. This may happen to a nucleus of a heavy element, e.g. the **isotope*** uranium-238, but the probability is very low compared to that of a simpler process like **alpha decay*** occurring instead.

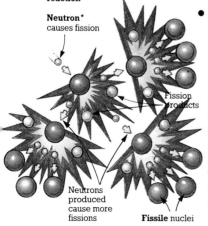

Induced fission causing **chain reaction**

Neutron* causes fission

Fission products

Neutrons produced cause more fissions

Fissile nuclei

• **Induced fission. Nuclear fission** of a nucleus made unstable by artificial means, i.e. by being hit by a fast particle (often a **neutron***), which it then absorbs. Not all nuclei can be induced to fission in this way; those which can, e.g. those of the **isotopes*** uranium-235 and plutonium-239, are described as **fissile**. If there are lots of fissile nuclei in a substance (see also **thermal** and **fast reactor**, page 95), the neutrons released by induced fissions will cause more fissions (and neutrons), and so on. This is known as a **chain reaction**. A well controlled chain reaction is allowed to occur in a **fission reactor***, but that occurring in a **fission bomb** is uncontrolled and extremely explosive.

* Alpha decay, 87; Fission reactor, 94; Isotopes, 83; Neutrons, 82; Radioactivity, 86.

- **Critical mass**. The minimum mass of a **fissile** substance needed to sustain a **chain reaction** (see **induced fission**). In smaller **subcritical masses**, the surface area to volume ratio is too high, and too many of the **neutrons*** produced by the first fissions escape into the atmosphere. Nuclear fuel is kept in subcritical masses.

- **Fission bomb** or **atom bomb (A-bomb)**. A bomb in which two **subcritical masses** (see above) are brought together by a trigger explosion. The resulting **chain reaction** (see **induced fission**) releases huge amounts of energy.

Critical mass

Small surface area (compared to volume)

Fast **neutron*** introduced to cause **nuclear fission**

Few neutrons escaping (most cause more fissions)

Chain reaction results

Subcritical mass

Large surface area (compared to volume)

Too many neutrons escaping (not enough cause more fissions)

No resulting chain reaction.

- **Nuclear fusion**. The collision and combination of two light nuclei to form a heavier, more stable nucleus, with the release of large amounts of energy (see also page 84). Unlike **nuclear fission**, it does not leave **radioactive*** products. Nuclear fusion requires temperatures of millions of degrees Celsius, to give the nuclei enough **kinetic energy*** for them to fuse when they collide (because of the high temperatures, fusion reactions are also called **thermonuclear reactions**). It therefore only occurs naturally in the sun (and stars like it), but research is being carried out with the aim of achieving controlled, induced fusion in **fusion reactors***.

- **Fusion bomb** or **hydrogen bomb (H-bomb)**. A bomb in which uncontrolled **nuclear fusion** occurs in a mixture of tritium and deuterium (hydrogen **isotopes***). A trigger **fission bomb** creates the high temperature needed (fusion bombs are also called **fission-fusion bombs**). The energy released is about 30 times that from a fission bomb of the same size.

Example of **nuclear fusion (D-T reaction** – see also **fusion reactor**, page 94)

Nuclear equation for reaction, left (see **mass** and **atomic numbers**, page 82):

$$^2_1H + ^3_1H \rightarrow ^4_2He + ^1_0n + energy$$

Deuterium nucleus (hydrogen **isotope***)

Tritium nucleus (hydrogen **isotope***)

Energy released (see page 84)

Single **neutron*** released

Fusion produces helium nucleus

Nuclei brought together at very high temperature

Hydrogen undergoes **nuclear fusion** in the sun.

Solar flare (jet of gas showing fusion activity).

---

* **Fusion reactor**, 94; **Isotopes**, 83; **Kinetic energy**, 9; **Neutrons**, 82; **Radioactivity**, 86.

Power from nuclear reactions

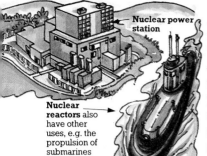

Nuclear power station

Nuclear reactors also have other uses, e.g. the propulsion of submarines and other ships.

A **nuclear reactor** is a structure inside which nuclear reactions produce vast amounts of heat. There are potentially two main types of reactor – **fission reactors** and **fusion reactors**, though the latter are still being researched. All present-day **nuclear power stations** are built around a central fission reactor and each generates, per unit mass of fuel, far larger amounts of power (electricity) than any other type of power station.

- **Fission reactor**. A **nuclear reactor** in which the heat is produced by **nuclear fission***. There are two main types in use in nuclear power stations – **thermal reactors** and **fast reactors** (see following page), both of which use uranium as their main fuel. This is held in long cylinders packed in the **core** (centre of the reactor). The rate of the **chain reaction*** (and hence power production) is closely controlled by **control rods**. See diagram below for the use of a fission reactor to generate power.

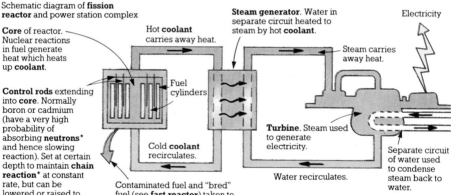

Schematic diagram of **fission reactor** and power station complex

Core of reactor. Nuclear reactions in fuel generate heat which heats up **coolant**.

Control rods extending into **core**. Normally boron or cadmium (have a very high probability of absorbing **neutrons*** and hence slowing reaction). Set at certain depth to maintain **chain reaction*** at constant rate, but can be lowered or raised to absorb more or fewer neutrons.

Hot **coolant** carries away heat.

Fuel cylinders

Cold **coolant** recirculates.

Contaminated fuel and "bred" fuel (see **fast reactor**) taken to **reprocessing plant**, where useful material is reclaimed.

Steam generator. Water in separate circuit heated to steam by hot **coolant**.

Steam carries away heat.

Turbine. Steam used to generate electricity.

Water recirculates.

Electricity

Separate circuit of water used to condense steam back to water.

- **Fusion reactor**. A type of **nuclear reactor**, being researched but as yet undeveloped, in which the heat would be produced by **nuclear fusion***. This would probably be the fusion of the nuclei of the hydrogen **isotopes*** deuterium and tritium – known as the **D-T reaction** (see picture, page 93). There are several major problems to be overcome before a fusion reactor becomes a reality, but it would produce about four times as much energy per unit mass of fuel as a **fission reactor**. Also, hydrogen is abundant, whereas uranium is scarce, and dangerous and expensive to mine.

Dangerous **radioactive*** waste (spent fuel) from **fission reactors** must be buried. **Fusion reactors** would not produce such waste.

* Chain reaction, 92 (Induced fission); Isotopes, 83; Neutrons, 82; Nuclear fission, 92; Nuclear fusion, 93; Radioactivity, 86.

Types of fission reactor

Thermal reactor. A **fission reactor** containing a **moderator** around the fuel cylinders. This is a substance with light nuclei, such as graphite or water. It is used to slow down the fast **neutrons*** produced by the first fissions in the uranium fuel – the neutrons bounce off the light nuclei (which themselves are unlikely to absorb neutrons) and eventually slow down to about 2200 m s⁻¹.

Slowing the neutrons improves their chances of causing further fissions (and continuing the **chain reaction***). Faster neutrons are likely to be "captured" by the most abundant nuclei – those of the **isotope*** uranium-238 (see **fast reactor**), whereas slow neutrons can travel on until they find uranium-235 nuclei. These will undergo fission when hit by neutrons of any speed, but make up a smaller percentage of the fuel (despite the fact that it is now often enriched with extra ^{235}U).

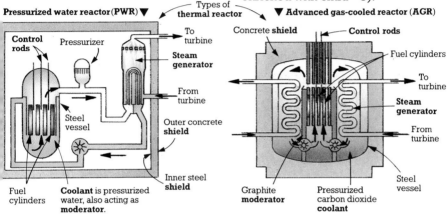

Pressurized water reactor (PWR) ▼

Types of thermal reactor

Advanced gas-cooled reactor (AGR) ▼

Control rods

Pressurizer

To turbine

Steam generator

From turbine

Steel vessel

Outer concrete shield

Inner steel shield

Fuel cylinders

Coolant is pressurized water, also acting as **moderator**.

Concrete **shield**

Control rods

Fuel cylinders

To turbine

Steam generator

From turbine

Steel vessel

Graphite **moderator**

Pressurized carbon dioxide **coolant**

• **Fast reactor** or **fast breeder reactor** **(FBR)**. A **fission reactor**, inside which the **neutrons*** which cause the fission are allowed to remain as fast neutrons (travelling at about 2×10^7 m s⁻¹). The fuel used is always enriched with extra nuclei of uranium-235 (see **thermal reactor**) and plutonium-239. Both of these will fission easily when hit by fast neutrons, unlike uranium-238, which is far more likely to "capture" the neutrons (becoming ^{239}U) and undergo **radioactive decay***. The final product of this decay, however, is ^{239}Pu. Fast reactors are also called "breeders" because this decay process of ^{239}U to ^{239}Pu is allowed to happen in a blanket of ^{238}U around the main fuel. Hence more fuel is created and can be stored.

Fast reactors have a more compact core and run at higher temperatures than thermal reactors. They are also more efficient, using up a much greater proportion of their fuel before it becomes contaminated.

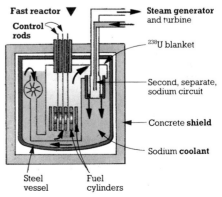

Fast reactor ▼

Control rods

Steam generator and turbine

^{238}U blanket

Second, separate, sodium circuit

Concrete **shield**

Sodium **coolant**

Steel vessel

Fuel cylinders

* **Chain reaction**, 92 (Induced fission); **Isotopes**, 83; **Neutrons**, 82; **Radioactive decay**, 87.

95

Quantities and units

Physical quantities are such things as **mass***, **force*** and **current***, which are used in the physical sciences. They all have to be measured in some way and each therefore has its own **unit**. These are chosen by international agreement and are called **International system** or **SI units** (abbreviated from the French Système International). All quantities are classified as either **basic quantities** or **derived quantities**.

• **Basic quantities.** A set of quantities from which all other quantities (see **derived quantities**) can be defined (see table, right). Each basic quantity has its **basic SI unit**, in terms of which any other SI unit can be defined.

Basic quantity	Symbol	Basic SI unit	Abbreviation
Mass	m	kilogram	kg
Length	l	metre	m
Time	t	second	s
Current	I	ampere	A
Temperature	T	kelvin	K
Quantity of substance	–	mole	mol
Luminous intensity	-	candela	cd

Basic SI units

• **Kilogram (kg).** The SI unit of mass. It is equal to the mass of an international prototype metal cylinder kept at Sèvres, near Paris.

• **Metre (m).** The SI unit of length. It is equal to the length of 1 650 763.73 **wavelengths*** of a certain type of radiation emitted by the krypton-86 atom.

• **Second (s).** The SI unit of time. It is equal to the duration of 9 192 631 770 **periods*** of a certain type of radiation emitted by the caesium-133 atom.

• **Ampere (A).** The SI unit of electric current (see also page 60). It is equal to the size of a current flowing through parallel, infinitely long, straight wires in a vacuum that produces a force between the wires of 2×10^{-7} N every metre.

• **Kelvin (K).** The SI unit of temperature. It is equal to 1/273.16 of the temperature of the **triple point** of water (the point at which ice, water and steam can all exist at the same time) on the **absolute temperature scale***.

• **Mole (mol).** The SI unit of the quantity of a substance (note that this is different from mass because it is the number of particles of a substance). It is equal to the amount of substance which contains 6.02×10^{23} (this is **Avagadro's number**) particles (e.g. atoms or molecules).

• **Candela (cd).** The SI unit of intensity of light. It is equal to the strength of light from 1/600 000 square metres of a **black body*** at the temperature of freezing platinum and at a pressure of 101 325 N m^{-2}.

Prefixes

A given SI unit may sometimes be too large or small for convenience, e.g. the metre is too large for measuring the thickness of a piece of paper. Standard fractions and multiples of the SI units are therefore used and are written by placing a prefix before the unit (see tables below and right). For example, the millimetre (mm) is equal to one thousandth of a metre.

Standard fractions and multiples (those involving powers of 10^3, e.g. 10^3, 10^6, 10^{-3}).

Fraction	Prefix	Symbol
10^{-3}	milli-	m
10^{-6}	micro-	μ
10^{-9}	nano-	n

Multiple	Prefix	Symbol
10^3	kilo-	k
10^6	mega-	M
10^9	giga-	G

Other fractions and multiples in use

Fraction or multiple	Prefix	Symbol
10^2	hecto-	h
10^1	deca-	dc
10^{-1}	deci-	d
10^{-2}	centi-	c

* Absolute temperature scale, 27; Black body, 29 (Leslie's cube); Current, 60; Force, 6; Mass, 12; Period, 16; Wavelength, 34.

• **Derived quantities.** Quantities other than **basic quantities** which are defined in terms of these or in terms of other derived quantities. The derived quantities have **derived SI units** which are defined in terms of the **basic SI units** or other derived units. They are worked out from the defining equation for the quantity and are sometimes given special names.

Derived quantity	Symbol	Defining equation	Derived SI unit	Name of unit	Abbreviation
Velocity	v	$v = \dfrac{\text{distance}}{\text{time}}$	$m\ s^{-1}$	-	-
Acceleration	a	$a = \dfrac{\text{velocity}}{\text{time}}$	$m\ s^{-2}$	-	-
Force	F	$F = \text{mass} \times \text{acceleration}$	$kg\ m\ s^{-2}$	newton	N
Work	W	$W = \text{force} \times \text{distance}$	$N\ m$	joule	J
Energy	E	Capacity to do work	J	-	-
Power	P	$P = \dfrac{\text{work done}}{\text{time}}$	$J\ s^{-1}$	watt	W
Area	A	Depends on shape (see page 101)	m^2	-	-
Volume	V	Depends on shape (see page 101)	m^3	-	-
Density	ρ	$\rho = \dfrac{\text{mass}}{\text{volume}}$	$kg\ m^{-3}$	-	-
Pressure	P	$P = \dfrac{\text{force}}{\text{area}}$	$N\ m^{-2}$	pascal	Pa
Period	T	Time for one cycle	s	-	-
Frequency	f	Number of cycles per second	s^{-1}	hertz	Hz
Impulse	-	$\text{Impulse} = \text{force} \times \text{time}$	$N\ s$	-	-
Momentum	-	$\text{Momentum} = \text{mass} \times \text{velocity}$	$kg\ m\ s^{-1}$	-	-
Electric charge	Q	$Q = \text{current} \times \text{time}$	$A\ s$	coulomb	C
Potential difference	V	$V = \dfrac{\text{energy transferred}}{\text{charge}}$	$J\ C^{-1}$	volt	V
Capacitance	C	$C = \dfrac{\text{charge}}{\text{potential difference}}$	$C\ V^{-1}$	farad	F
Resistance	R	$R = \dfrac{\text{potential difference}}{\text{current}}$	$V\ A^{-1}$	ohm	Ω

Equations, symbols and graphs

All **physical quantities** (see pages 96-97) and their units can be represented by **symbols** and are normally dependent on other quantities in some way. There is therefore a relationship between them which can be expressed as an **equation** and shown on a **graph**.

Equations

An **equation** represents the relationship between two or more physical quantities. This relationship can be expressed as a **word equation** or as an equation relating **symbols** which represent the quantities. The second case is used when a number of quantities are involved, since it is then easier to manipulate. Note that the meaning of the symbols must be stated.

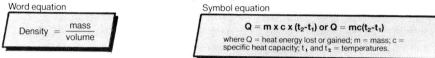

Word equation

$$\text{Density} = \frac{\text{mass}}{\text{volume}}$$

Symbol equation

$$Q = m \times c \times (t_2 - t_1) \text{ or } Q = mc(t_2 - t_1)$$

where Q = heat energy lost or gained; m = mass; c = specific heat capacity; t_1 and t_2 = temperatures.

Graphs

A **graph** is a visual representation of the relationship between two quantities. It shows how one quantity depends on another. Points on a graph are plotted using the values for the quantities obtained during an experiment or by using the equation for the relationship if it is known. The two quantities plotted are called the **variables**.

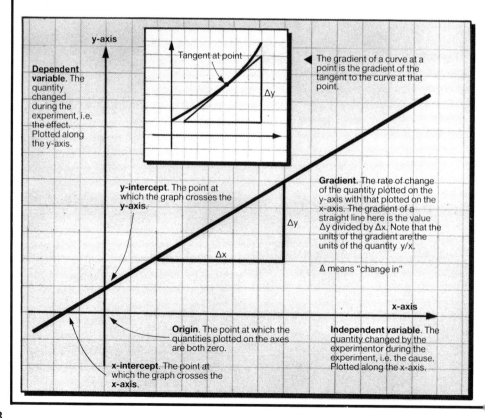

y-axis

Dependent variable. The quantity changed during the experiment, i.e. the effect. Plotted along the y-axis.

Tangent at point

The gradient of a curve at a point is the gradient of the tangent to the curve at that point.

Δy

y-intercept. The point at which the graph crosses the **y-axis.**

Gradient. The rate of change of the quantity plotted on the y-axis with that plotted on the x-axis. The gradient of a straight line here is the value Δy divided by Δx. Note that the units of the gradient are the units of the quantity y/x.

Δy

Δx

Δ means "change in"

x-axis

Origin. The point at which the quantities plotted on the axes are both zero.

Independent variable. The quantity changed by the experimenter during the experiment, i.e. the cause. Plotted along the x-axis.

x-intercept. The point at which the graph crosses the **x-axis.**

Symbols

Symbols are used to represent **physical quantities**. The value of a physical quantity consists of a numerical value and its unit. Therefore any symbol represents both a number and a unit.

Symbols represent number and unit

m = 2.1 kg   s = 400 J kg^{-1} K^{-1}

"Current through resistor = I" (i.e. do not need to say I amps since the unit is included)

Note that a symbol divided by a unit is a pure number.

m = 2.1 kg means that m/kg = 2.1

This notation is used in tables and to label graph axes.

Any number in this column is a length in metres.

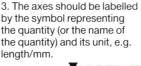

l/m	t²/s²
0.9	3.6
1.0	4.0
1.1	4.4
1.2	4.8

Any number in this column is a time squared measured in seconds squared.

Any number on scale is a force in newtons.

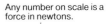
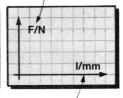

Any number on scale is a length in millimetres.

Plotting graphs

1. The quantity controlled during an experiment should be plotted along the x-axis and the quantity which changes as a result along the y-axis.

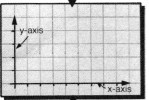

2. The scales on the axes should be chosen so that values are easy to find (squares on the paper representing multiples of three should be avoided).

3. The axes should be labelled by the symbol representing the quantity (or the name of the quantity) and its unit, e.g. length/mm.

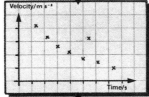

4. Points on the graph should be marked in pencil with a **x** or a ⊙.

5. A smooth curve or straight line should be drawn which fits the points best (this is because physical quantities normally are related in some

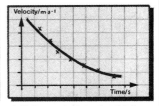

definite way). Note that joining the points up will not often produce a smooth curve. This is due to experimental errors.

Information from graphs

A straight line graph which passes through the origin shows that the quantities plotted on the graph are proportional to each other (i.e. if one is doubled then so is the other).

The amount of scatter of the points about the smooth curve gives an indication of the errors in the data due to inaccuracies in the procedure, the equipment and the measuring (this happens in any experiment).

A graph shows the region in which the relationship between two quantities is linear (i.e. one always changes by the same amount for a fixed change in the other). It is that in which the graph is a straight line.

Individual points a long way from the curve are probably due to an error in measuring that piece of data in the experiment. However, the point should not be ignored – it should be checked and re-measured if possible.

Measurements

Measurement of length

The method used to measure a length depends on the magnitude of the length. A metre rule is used for lengths of 50 mm or more. The smallest division is normally 1 mm and so lengths can be estimated to the nearest 0.5 mm. For lengths less than 50 mm, the error involved would be unacceptable (see also **reading error**, page 103). A **vernier scale** is therefore used. For the measurement of very small lengths (to 0.01 mm) a **micrometer screw gauge** is used.

- **Vernier scale.** A short scale which slides along a fixed scale. The position on the fixed scale of the zero line of the vernier scale can be found accurately. It is used in measuring devices such as the **vernier slide callipers**.

Method of reading position of zero line on **vernier scale**:

1. Read the position of the zero line approximately – in this case 8.3 cm.

2. Find the position on the vernier scale where the marks coincide – in this case 2.

3. Add this to the previous figure – the accurate reading is 8.32 cm.

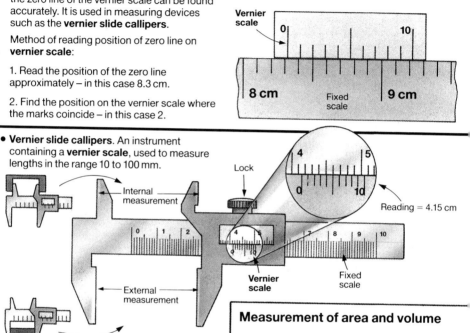

- **Vernier slide callipers.** An instrument containing a **vernier scale**, used to measure lengths in the range 10 to 100 mm.

Reading = 4.15 cm

Method of measurement:

1. Close the jaws and check that the zero on the **vernier scale** coincides with the zero on the fixed scale. If not, note the reading (this is the **zero error***).

2. Close or open the jaws onto the object to be measured.

3. Lock the sliding jaw into position.

4. Record the reading on the scale.

5. Add or subtract the zero error (see 1) to get the correct reading.

Measurement of area and volume

The volume of a liquid is calculated from the space it takes up in its containing vessel. The internal volume of the containing vessel is called its **capacity**. The **SI unit*** of capacity is the **litre (l)**, equal to 10^{-3} m^3. Note that 1 ml = 1 cm^3. The volume of a liquid is measured using a graduated vessel.

Examples of graduated vessels for measuring volume

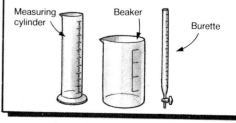

 * SI units, 96; Zero error, 102.

- **Micrometer screw gauge.** An instrument used for accurate measurements up to about 30 mm.

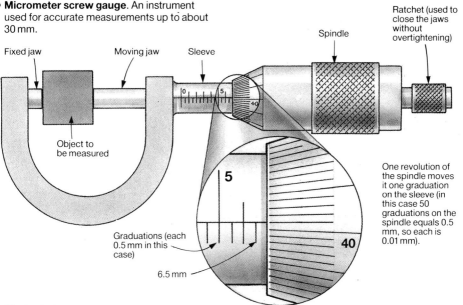

Fixed jaw

Moving jaw

Sleeve

Spindle

Ratchet (used to close the jaws without overtightening)

Object to be measured

5

Graduations (each 0.5 mm in this case)

6.5 mm

40

One revolution of the spindle moves it one graduation on the sleeve (in this case 50 graduations on the spindle equals 0.5 mm, so each is 0.01 mm).

Method of measurement

1. Work out the value of a division on the spindle scale (see diagram).

2. Using the ratchet, close the jaws of the instrument fully. The zero on the spindle scale should coincide with the horizontal reference line. If not, note the **zero error***.

3. Using the ratchet, close the jaws on the object to be measured until it is gripped.

4. Note the reading of the highest visible mark on the sleeve scale (in this case 6.5 mm).

5. Note the division on the spindle scale which coincides with the horizontal reference line (in this case 0.41 mm).

6. Add the two readings and add or subtract the zero error (see 2) to get the correct reading (in this case 6.91 mm).

The surface area and volume of a solid of regular shape are calculated from length measurements of the object (see below).

For solids of irregular shape, see **eureka can**, page 24.

Regular shaped solid	Rectangular bar	Sphere	Cylinder
Measurements made using **vernier slide callipers** or **micrometer screw gauge**	h = height b = breadth l = length	r = radius	r = radius l = length
Volume v of solid calculated from	$v = lbh$	$v = 4/3\,\pi r^3$	$v = \pi r^2 l$
Surface area a calculated from	$a = 2bl + 2hl + 2hb$ ↑ Top ↑ Sides ↑ Ends	$a = 4\pi r^2$	$a = 2\pi rl + 2\pi r^2$ ↑ Curved surface ↑ Ends

* **Zero error**, 102.

Accuracy and errors

All experimental measurements are subject to some errors, other than those caused by carelessness (like misreading a scale). The most common errors which occur are **parallax errors**, **zero errors** and **reading errors**. When stating a reading, therefore, a number of **significant figures** should be quoted which give an estimate of the accuracy of the readings.

- **Parallax error.** The error which occurs when the eye is not placed directly opposite a scale when a reading is being taken.

Correct reading of 31.45 when eye vertically above mark to be read

Parallax error
reading metre rule

Parallax error – reading 31.40

Parallax error – reading 31.50

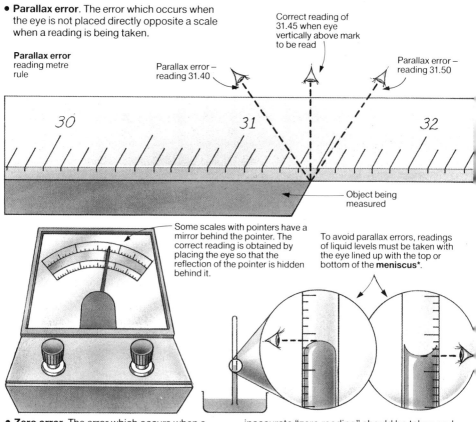

Object being measured

Some scales with pointers have a mirror behind the pointer. The correct reading is obtained by placing the eye so that the reflection of the pointer is hidden behind it.

To avoid parallax errors, readings of liquid levels must be taken with the eye lined up with the top or bottom of the **meniscus***.

- **Zero error.** The error which occurs when a measuring instrument does not indicate zero when it should. If this happens, the instrument should either be adjusted to read zero or the inaccurate "zero reading" should be taken and should be added to or subtracted from any other reading taken.

Reading on **vernier slide callipers*** when closed (i.e. should read zero) is 0.2 mm. This is **zero error**.

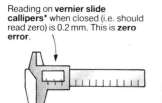

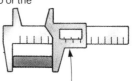

0.2 mm must be subtracted from any reading (in this case, apparent reading is 53.9 but actual length is 53.9 – 0.2, i.e. 53.7 mm)

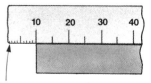

Zero error on metre rule may be due to worn end. Should be solved by measuring from 10 mm line and subtracting 10 mm from all readings.

- **Reading error.** The error due to the guesswork involved in taking a reading from a scale when the reading lies between the scale divisions.

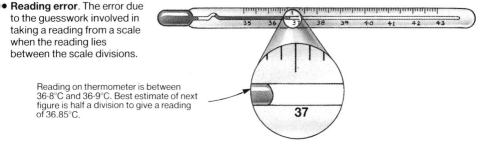

Reading on thermometer is between 36·8°C and 36·9°C. Best estimate of next figure is half a division to give a reading of 36.85°C.

Significant figures

The number of **significant figures** in a value is the number of figures in that value ignoring leading or trailing zeros (but see below) and disregarding the position of the decimal point. They give an indication of the accuracy of a reading.

A reading of 3704 mm has four **significant figures**. It can be written as:

3 704 mm

3.704 m

0.003 704 km

4th significant figure

1st significant figure

Note that the leading zeros here are not significant figures but show the magnitude of the reading.

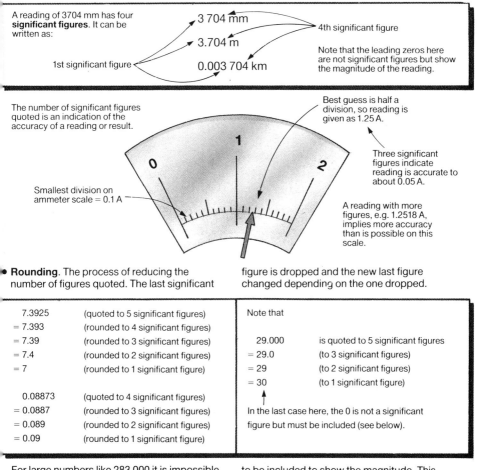

The number of significant figures quoted is an indication of the accuracy of a reading or result.

Best guess is half a division, so reading is given as 1.25 A.

Three significant figures indicate reading is accurate to about 0.05 A.

Smallest division on ammeter scale = 0.1 A

A reading with more figures, e.g. 1.2518 A, implies more accuracy than is possible on this scale.

- **Rounding.** The process of reducing the number of figures quoted. The last significant figure is dropped and the new last figure changed depending on the one dropped.

7.3925	(quoted to 5 significant figures)
= 7.393	(rounded to 4 significant figures)
= 7.39	(rounded to 3 significant figures)
= 7.4	(rounded to 2 significant figures)
= 7	(rounded to 1 significant figure)

0.08873	(quoted to 4 significant figures)
= 0.0887	(rounded to 3 significant figures)
= 0.089	(rounded to 2 significant figures)
= 0.09	(rounded to 1 significant figure)

Note that

29.000	is quoted to 5 significant figures
= 29.0	(to 3 significant figures)
= 29	(to 2 significant figures)
= 30	(to 1 significant figure)

↑

In the last case here, the 0 is not a significant figure but must be included (see below).

For large numbers like 283 000 it is impossible to say how many of the figures are significant (the first three must be) because the zeros have to be included to show the magnitude. This ambiguity is removed by using the **index notation** (see page 109).

Fields and forces

This table is a comparison of the three forces normally encountered in physics (excluding the **nuclear force**). In fact, most of the forces dealt with in physics, e.g. the **contact force** between two objects, are examples of the **electromagnetic force** which is a combination of the **magnetic** and **electric forces**. For more about these and all other forces, see pages 6-7.

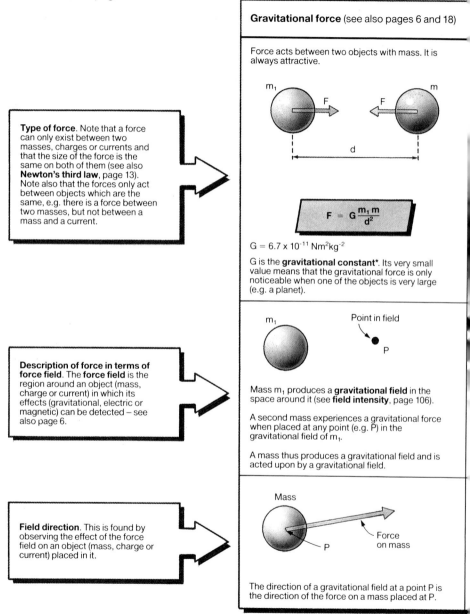

Gravitational force (see also pages 6 and 18)

Force acts between two objects with mass. It is always attractive.

m_1 m

F   F

d

Type of force. Note that a force can only exist between two masses, charges or currents and that the size of the force is the same on both of them (see also **Newton's third law**, page 13). Note also that the forces only act between objects which are the same, e.g. there is a force between two masses, but not between a mass and a current.

$$F = G\frac{m_1 m}{d^2}$$

$G = 6.7 \times 10^{-11}\ \text{Nm}^2\text{kg}^{-2}$

G is the **gravitational constant***. Its very small value means that the gravitational force is only noticeable when one of the objects is very large (e.g. a planet).

m_1 Point in field

P

Description of force in terms of force field. The **force field** is the region around an object (mass, charge or current) in which its effects (gravitational, electric or magnetic) can be detected – see also page 6.

Mass m_1 produces a **gravitational field** in the space around it (see **field intensity**, page 106).

A second mass experiences a gravitational force when placed at any point (e.g. P) in the gravitational field of m_1.

A mass thus produces a gravitational field and is acted upon by a gravitational field.

Mass

Field direction. This is found by observing the effect of the force field on an object (mass, charge or current) placed in it.

Force on mass

P

The direction of a gravitational field at a point P is the direction of the force on a mass placed at P.

* Gravitational constant, 18 (Newton's law of gravitation).

Electric force (see also pages 6 and 58)	**Magnetic force** (see also pages 6 and 70)

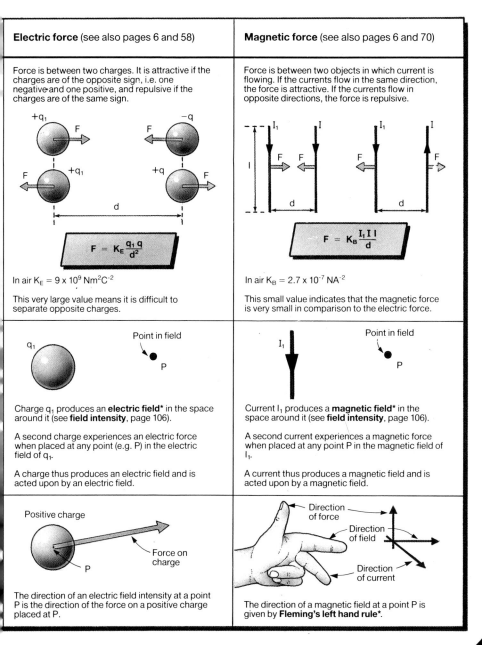

Electric force (see also pages 6 and 58)

Force is between two charges. It is attractive if the charges are of the opposite sign, i.e. one negative and one positive, and repulsive if the charges are of the same sign.

$$F = K_E \frac{q_1 q}{d^2}$$

In air $K_E = 9 \times 10^9$ Nm^{2}C^{-2}

This very large value means it is difficult to separate opposite charges.

Point in field
P

Charge q_1 produces an **electric field*** in the space around it (see **field intensity**, page 106).

A second charge experiences an electric force when placed at any point (e.g. P) in the electric field of q_1.

A charge thus produces an electric field and is acted upon by an electric field.

Positive charge

Force on charge
P

The direction of an electric field intensity at a point P is the direction of the force on a positive charge placed at P.

Magnetic force (see also pages 6 and 70)

Force is between two objects in which current is flowing. If the currents flow in the same direction, the force is attractive. If the currents flow in opposite directions, the force is repulsive.

$$F = K_B \frac{I_1 I l}{d}$$

In air $K_B = 2.7 \times 10^{-7}$ NA^{-2}

This small value indicates that the magnetic force is very small in comparison to the electric force.

Point in field
P

Current I_1 produces a **magnetic field*** in the space around it (see **field intensity**, page 106).

A second current experiences a magnetic force when placed at any point P in the magnetic field of I_1.

A current thus produces a magnetic field and is acted upon by a magnetic field.

Direction of force
Direction of field
Direction of current

The direction of a magnetic field at a point P is given by **Fleming's left hand rule***.

* Electric field, 58; Fleming's left hand rule, 76; Magnetic field, 72.

Fields and forces (continued)

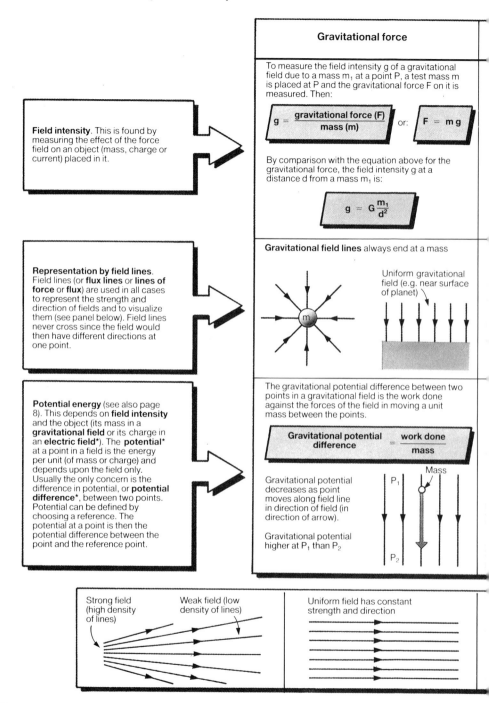

Gravitational force

To measure the field intensity g of a gravitational field due to a mass m_1 at a point P, a test mass m is placed at P and the gravitational force F on it is measured. Then:

$$g = \frac{\text{gravitational force (F)}}{\text{mass (m)}} \quad \text{or:} \quad F = mg$$

By comparison with the equation above for the gravitational force, the field intensity g at a distance d from a mass m_1 is:

$$g = G\frac{m_1}{d^2}$$

Field intensity. This is found by measuring the effect of the force field on an object (mass, charge or current) placed in it.

Gravitational field lines always end at a mass

Uniform gravitational field (e.g. near surface of planet)

Representation by field lines. Field lines (or **flux lines** or **lines of force** or **flux**) are used in all cases to represent the strength and direction of fields and to visualize them (see panel below). Field lines never cross since the field would then have different directions at one point.

The gravitational potential difference between two points in a gravitational field is the work done against the forces of the field in moving a unit mass between the points.

$$\text{Gravitational potential difference} = \frac{\text{work done}}{\text{mass}}$$

Gravitational potential decreases as point moves along field line in direction of field (in direction of arrow).

Gravitational potential higher at P_1 than P_2

Mass
P_1
P_2

Potential energy (see also page 8). This depends on **field intensity** and the object (its mass in a **gravitational field** or its charge in an **electric field***). The **potential*** at a point in a field is the energy per unit (of mass or charge) and depends upon the field only. Usually the only concern is the difference in potential, or **potential difference***, between two points. Potential can be defined by choosing a reference. The potential at a point is then the potential difference between the point and the reference point.

Strong field (high density of lines)

Weak field (low density of lines)

Uniform field has constant strength and direction

* Electric field, Potential, Potential difference, 58.

Electric force	Magnetic force
To measure the field intensity E of an electric field at a point P due to a charge q_1, a test positive charge q is placed at P and the electric force F on it is measured. Then:	To measure the field intensity B of a magnetic field due to I_1 at a point P, a conductor of length l carrying a current I is placed at P and the magnetic force F is measured. Then:

$$E = \frac{\text{electric force (F)}}{\text{charge (q)}}$$ or: $$F = qE$$

$$B = \frac{\text{magnetic force (F)}}{\text{current (I)} \times \text{length (l)}}$$ or: $$F = BIl$$

By comparison with the equation above for the electric force, the field intensity E at a distance d from a charge q_1 is:	By comparison with the equation above for the magnetic force, the field intensity B at a distance d from a current I_1 is:

$$E = K_E \frac{q_1}{d^2}$$

$$B = K_B \frac{I_1}{d}$$

Electric field lines always begin at a positive charge and end at an equal negative charge.	**Magnetic field lines*** have no beginning or end, but are always closed loops. This is because single north or south poles cannot exist. This is a fundamental difference compared to gravitational and electric fields.

Circular magnetic field lines around current-carrying wire.

The electric potential difference between two points in an electric field is the work done against the forces of the field in moving a unit positive between them.	

$$\text{Electric potential difference} = \frac{\text{work done}}{\text{charge}}$$

Electric potential decreases as point moves along field line in direction of field (in direction of arrow). Electric potential higher at point P_1 than at P_2	Magnetic potential is much more difficult to define than for gravitational or electric fields because the field lines are circular. Note that if a point moves around a circular line in the diagram above, it returns to the same point, which must have the same potential, although it has moved along a field line. This means that magnetic potential is complicated to calculate.

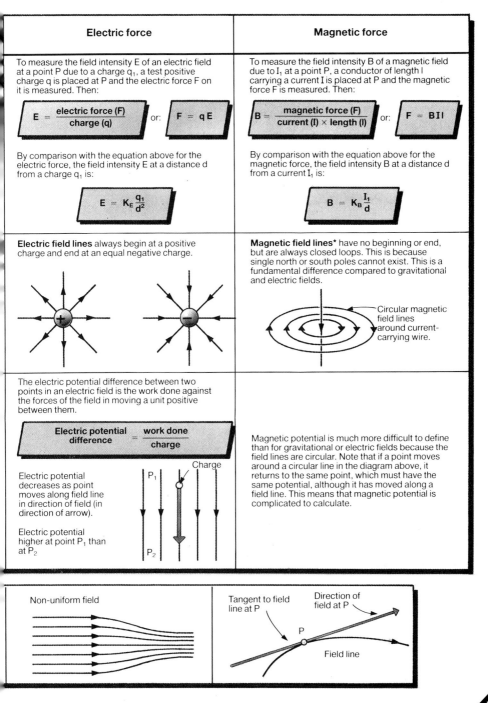

Non-uniform field

Tangent to field line at P

Direction of field at P

P

Field line

Vectors and scalars

All quantities in physics are either **scalar** or **vector quantities**, depending on whether the quantity has direction as well as magnitude.

- **Scalar quantity**. Any quantity which has magnitude only, e.g. mass, time, energy, density.

- **Vector quantity**. Any quantity which has both magnitude and direction, e.g. force, displacement, velocity and acceleration. When giving a value to a vector quantity, the direction must be given in some way as well as the magnitude. Usually, the quantity is represented graphically by an arrowed line. The length of the line indicates the magnitude of the quantity (on some chosen scale) and the direction of the arrow the direction of the quantity.

- **Parallelogram rule**. A rule used when adding together two **vector quantities**. The two vectors are drawn from one point to form two sides of a parallelogram which is then completed. The diagonal from the original common point gives the sum of the two vectors (the **resultant**).

Arrows represent forces (**vector quantities**). Length indicates magnitude of force.

Forces act in opposite directions

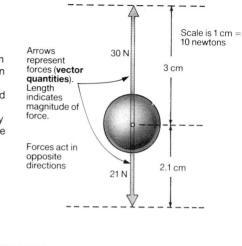

Scale is 1 cm = 10 newtons

30 N

3 cm

21 N

2.1 cm

The **parallelogram rule** is used to help navigation at sea. The direction and speed of the tide must be taken into account as the second **vector quantity** to be added to the direction and speed of the boat.

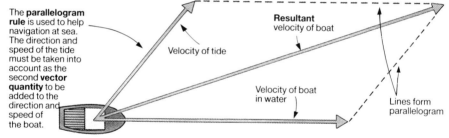

Velocity of tide

Resultant velocity of boat

Velocity of boat in water

Lines form parallelogram

- **Resolution**. The process of splitting one **vector quantity** into two other vectors called its **components**. Normally, the two components are perpendicular to each other. Each component then represents the total effect of the vector in that direction.

Lift (**vector quantity**) from rotor of helicopter can be **resolved** into two **components**. The first acts upwards, in order to keep it airborne, and the second acts forwards, to move it along.

First component is upward force (F x **sine*** θ)

Lift F

Second component is forward force (F x **cosine*** θ)

θ

Numbers

Very large or very small numbers (e.g. 10 000 000 or 0.000 001) take a long time to write out and are difficult to read. The **index notation** is therefore used. In this notation, the position of the decimal point is shown by writing the power ten is raised to.

1 000 000	$= 10^6$	or "ten to the six"
100 000	$= 10^5$	or "ten to the five"
10 000	$= 10^4$	or "ten to the four"
1 000	$= 10^3$	or "ten to the three"
100	$= 10^2$	or "ten to the two"
10	$= 10^1$	or "ten to the one"
1	$= 10^0$	any number "to the nought" equals one
0.1	$= 10^{-1}$	or "ten to the minus one"
0.01	$= 10^{-2}$	or "ten to the minus two"
0.001	$= 10^{-3}$	or "ten to the minus three"
0.000 1	$= 10^{-4}$	or "ten to the minus four"
0.000 01	$= 10^{-5}$	or "ten to the minus five"
0.000 001	$= 10^{-6}$	or "ten to the minus six"

Note that a negative index means "one over" so that $10^{-3} = 1/10^3 = 1/1000$. This also applies to units, e.g. $kg\ m^{-3}$ means kg/m^3 or kg per m^3.

Indices are added when multiplying numbers, e.g. $10^5 \times 10^{-3}$ ($= 100000 \times 1/1000$) $= 10^{5-3} = 10^2 = 100$

- **Standard form.** A form of expressing numbers in which the number always has one digit before the decimal point and is followed by a power of ten in **index notation** to show its magnitude (see also **significant figures**, page 103).

Examples of numbers written in **standard form**.

56342	5.6342×10^4
4000	4×10^3 (assuming 0s are not significant)
23.3	2.33×10^1
0.98	9.8×10^{-1}
0.00211	2.11×10^{-3}

- **Order of magnitude.** A value which is accurate to within a factor of ten or so. It is important to have an idea of the order of magnitude of some physical quantities so that a figure which has been calculated can be judged. For example, the mass of a person is about 60 kg. Therefore a calculated result of 50 kg or 70 kg is quite reasonable, but a result of 6 kg or 600 kg is obviously not correct.

Typical orders of magnitude

Item	Mass / kg
Earth	5×10^{24}
Car	5×10^3
Human	5×10^1
Bag of sugar	1
Orange	2×10^{-1}
Golf ball	5×10^{-2}
Table-tennis ball	2×10^{-3}
Proton	2×10^{-27}
Electron	10^{-30}

Item	Length / m
Radius of galaxy	10^{19}
Radius of solar system	10^{11}
Radius of earth	5×10^6
Height of Mount Everest	10^4
Height of human	2
Thickness of paper	10^{-4}
Wavelength of light	5×10^{-7}
Radius of atom	10^{-10}
Radius of nucleus	10^{-14}

Item	Time / s
Age of earth	2×10^{17}
Time since emergence of man	10^{13}
Human life time	2×10^9
Time span of year	3×10^7
Time span of day	9×10^4
Time between heart beats	1
Camera shutter speed	10^{-2}
Half life of Polonium-214	1.5×10^{-4}
Time for light to travel 1 m	3×10^{-9}

Item	Energy / J
Energy given out by sun per second	10^{26}
Energy released by San Francisco earthquake (1906)	3×10^{17}
Energy released by fission of 1 g of uranium	10^{11}
Energy of lightning discharge	10^9
Energy of 1 kW fire per hour	4×10^6
Kinetic energy of golf ball	20

Circuit symbols

This table shows the main symbols used to represent the various components used in electric circuits (see also pages 60-65).

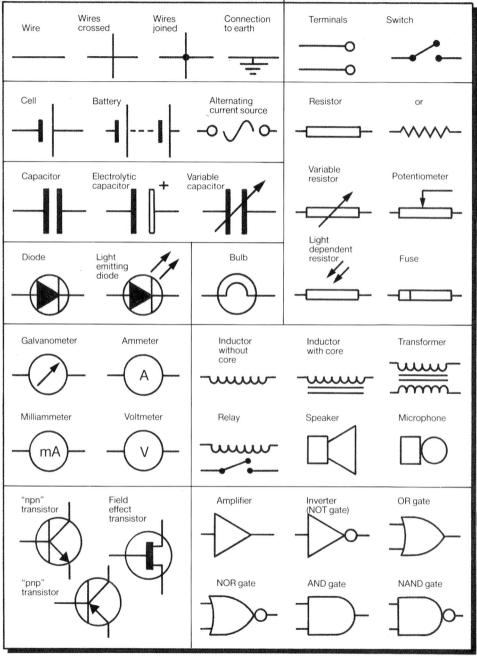

Transistors and gates

Transistors* can be used to amplify electrical signals, such as those from a microphone, and are also used as electronic switches. This has led to their use in complex circuits such as computers. They have replaced the much larger and slower valves and **relays***.

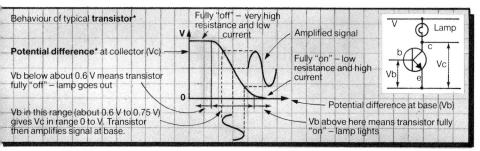

Behaviour of typical **transistor***

Potential difference* at collector (Vc)

Vb below about 0.6 V means transistor fully "off" – lamp goes out

Vb in this range (about 0.6 V to 0.75 V) gives Vc in range 0 to V. Transistor then amplifies signal at base.

Fully "off" – very high resistance and low current

Amplified signal

Fully "on" – low resistance and high current

Potential difference at base (Vb)

Vb above here means transistor fully "on" – lamp lights

V Lamp
b c
Vb Vc
e

Logic gates

The on and off states of a transistor are used to indicate the numbers 0 and 1. The circuits are therefore known as **digital** (other circuits are called **analogue**). Combinations of transistors with other components are used to make circuits which carry out logical operations.

Truth tables for basic logical operations

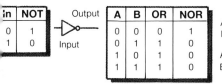

in	NOT
0	1
1	0

Output
Input

A	B	OR	NOR
0	0	0	1
0	1	1	0
1	0	1	0
1	1	1	0

Inputs
A
B OR

A
B NOR

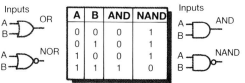

A	B	AND	NAND
0	0	0	1
0	1	0	1
1	0	0	1
1	1	1	0

Inputs
A
B AND

A
B NAND

Combinations of these gates and other transistor circuits are used to make complex circuits which can perform mathematical operations, e.g. addition. These are called **integrated circuits**, and may contain many thousands of such components and connections, yet be built into a single slice of silicon.

Computers

Integrated circuits mean that many thousands of logic gates can be put onto a single tiny component called a microchip. The CPU of a computer (see below) can be put on one chip.

Typical computer system

Disk drives are examples of **input** and **output** devices. The disks can store many times more data than the **memory**, and also retain it when the computer is turned off (the information in the **read only memory** is lost).

Devices such as a keyboard and screen are also **input** and **output** devices, from which data is put into the computer and to which it is sent. They are ways for the computer to link with the outside world.

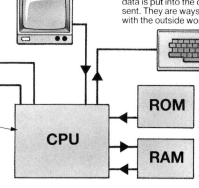

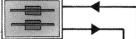

Central processing unit (CPU). The centre of the computer. It takes data from **memory** and **input** devices, performs operations on it (it can do this millions of times per second) and sends the results to memory or **output** devices.

Memory. The section of computer where the instructions (or program) for the **central processing unit** and the data are held. There are two types, **random access memory (RAM)**, where data can be stored (written) and retrieved (read), and **read only memory (ROM)**, from which "prerecorded" data can only be read.

ROM

CPU

RAM

Elements

Element	Symbol	Atomic number	Approximate r.a.m.*
Actinium	Ac	89	227
Aluminium	Al	13	27
Americium	Am	95	243
Antimony	Sb	51	122
Argon	Ar	18	40
Arsenic	As	33	75
Astatine	At	85	210
Barium	Ba	56	137
Beryllium	Be	4	9
Bismuth	Bi	83	209
Boron	B	5	11
Bromine	Br	35	80
Cadmium	Cd	48	112
Caesium	Cs	55	133
Calcium	Ca	20	40
Carbon	C	6	12
Cerium	Ce	58	140
Chlorine	Cl	17	35.5
Chromium	Cr	24	52
Cobalt	Co	27	59
Copper	Cu	29	64
Dysprosium	Dy	66	162
Erbium	Er	68	167
Europium	Eu	63	152
Fluorine	F	9	19
Francium	Fr	87	223
Gadolinium	Gd	64	157
Gallium	Ga	31	70
Germanium	Ge	32	73
Gold	Au	79	197
Hafnium	Hf	72	178.5
Helium	He	2	4
Holmium	Ho	67	165
Hydrogen	H	1	1
Indium	In	49	115
Iodine	I	53	127
Iridium	Ir	77	192
Iron	Fe	26	56
Krypton	Kr	36	84
Lanthanum	La	57	139
Lead	Pb	82	207
Lithium	Li	3	7
Lutetium	Lu	71	175
Magnesium	Mg	12	24
Manganese	Mn	25	55
Mercury	Hg	80	201
Molybdenum	Mo	42	96
Neodymium	Nd	60	144
Neon	Ne	10	20
Neptunium	Np	93	237
Nickel	Ni	28	59
Niobium	Nb	41	93
Nitrogen	N	7	14
Osmium	Os	76	190
Oxygen	O	8	16
Palladium	Pd	46	106
Phosphorus	P	15	31
Platinum	Pt	78	195
Plutonium	Pu	94	242
Polonium	Po	84	210
Potassium	K	19	39
Praseodymium	Pr	59	141
Promethium	Pm	61	147
Protactinium	Pa	91	231

Element	Symbol	Atomic number	Approximate r.a.m.*
Radium	Ra	88	226
Radon	Rn	86	222
Rhenium	Re	75	186
Rhodium	Rh	45	103
Rubidium	Rb	37	85
Ruthenium	Ru	44	101
Samarium	Sm	62	150
Scandium	Sc	21	45
Selenium	Se	34	79
Silicon	Si	14	28
Silver	Ag	47	108
Sodium	Na	11	23
Strontium	Sr	38	88
Sulphur	S	16	32
Tantalum	Ta	73	181
Technetium	Tc	43	99
Tellurium	Te	52	128
Terbium	Tb	65	159
Thallium	Tl	81	204
Thorium	Th	90	232
Thulium	Tm	69	169
Tin	Sn	50	119
Titanium	Ti	22	48
Tungsten	W	74	184
Uranium	U	92	238
Vanadium	V	23	51
Xenon	Xe	54	131
Ytterbium	Yb	70	173
Yttrium	Y	39	89
Zinc	Zn	30	65
Zirconium	Zr	40	91

* Relative atomic mass (r.a.m.), 83.

Useful constants

Quantity	Symbol	Value
Speed of light in vacuum	c	2.998×10^8 m s^{-1}
Charge on electron	e	1.602×10^{-19} C
Mass of electron	me	9.109×10^{-31} kg
Mass of proton	mp	1.673×10^{-27} kg
Mass of neutron	mn	1.675×10^{-27} kg
Avagadro's number	NA	6.023×10^{23} mol^{-1}
Faraday's constant	F	9.65×10^4 C mol^{-1}
Gravitational constant	G	6.670×10^{-11} N m^2 kg^{-2}
Gas constant	R	8.314 J mol^{-1} K^{-1}

Values of common quantities

Quantity	Value
Acceleration due to gravity g (gravitational field strength)	9.81 m s^{-2}
Density of water	1.00×10^3 kg m^{-3}
Density of mercury	13.6×10^3 kg m^{-3}
Ice point (standard temperature)	273 K
Steam point	373 K
Standard atmospheric pressure	1.01×10^5 Pa
Length of earth day	8.64×10^4 s

Properties of substances

(Density, specific heat capacity and resistivity all change with temperature. Values quoted here are for room temperature, i.e. 18–22°C.)

Substance	Density /10³ kg m⁻³	Young's modulus /10¹⁰ N m⁻²	Specific heat capacity /J kg⁻¹ K⁻¹	Specific latent heat of fusion /10⁴ J kg⁻¹	Linear expansivity /10⁻⁶ K⁻¹	Thermal conductivity /W m⁻¹ K⁻¹	Resistivity /10⁻⁸ ρ m
Aluminium	2.70	7.0	908	40.0	25	242	2.67
Antimony	6.62	7.8	210	16.5	11	19	44
Arsenic	5.73	–	335	–	6.0	–	33.3
Bismuth	9.78	3.2	112	5.5	14	9	117
Brass	8.6 (approx)	9.0	389	–	19	109	8 (approx)
Cadmium	8.65	5.0	230	5.5	30	96	–
Cobalt	8.70	–	435	24.0	12	93	6.4
Constantan	8.90	–	420	–	16	23	49
Copper	8.89	11.0	385	20.0	16	383	1.72
Gallium	5.93	–	377	–	19	34	17.4
Germanium	5.40	–	324	–	5.7	59	4.6×10^7
Gold	19.3	8.0	128	6.7	14	300	2.20
Iridium	22.4	–	135	–	6.5	59	5.2
Iron (cast)	7.60	11.0	460	21.0	12	71	10.3
Iron (wrought)	7.85	21.0					
Lead	11.3	1.6	127	2.5	29	36	20.6
Magnesium	1.74	4.1	1030	30.0	26	154	4.24
Mercury	13.6	–	139	1.2	12	9	95.9
Molybdenum	10.1	–	301	–	5.0	142	5.7
Nickel	8.80	21.0	456	29.0	13	59	6.94
Palladium	12.2	–	247	15.0	12	74	10.7
Platinum	21.5	17.0	135	11.5	9.0	71	10.5
Selenium	4.79	–	324	35.0	26	.24	10^{12} (approx)
Silicon (amorphous)	2.35	11.3	706	–	2.5	175	10^{10} (approx)
Silver	10.5	7.7	234	10.5	19	414	1.63
Steel (mild)	7.80	22.0	450	–	12	46	15 (approx)
Tantalum	16.6	19.0	151	–	6.5	56	13.4
Tellurium	6.2	–	201	–	17	50	1.6×10^5
Tin	7.3	5.3	225	5.8	23	63	11.4
Tungsten	19.3	39.0	142	–	4.3	185	5.5
Water	1.00	–	4200	33.4	33.4	.2	–
Zinc	7.10	8.0	387	10.5	11	111	5.92

Glossary

- **Alloy**. A mixture of two or more metals or a metal and a non-metal. It has its own properties (which are metallic), independent of those of its constituents. For example, brass is an alloy of copper and zinc, steel is an alloy of iron and carbon (different mixes give the steel different properties).

- **Calibration**. The "setting up" of a measuring instrument so that it gives the correct reading. The instrument is normally adjusted during manufacture so that it reads the correct value when it is measuring a known standard quantity, e.g. a balance would be adjusted to read exactly 1 kg when a standard 1 kg mass was on it.

- **Calorimetry**. The measurement of heat change during a chemical reaction or event involving heat transfer. For example, measuring the temperature rise of a known mass of a substance when it is heated electrically is used to find **specific heat capacity*** and the temperature rise of a mass of water can be used to calculate the energy produced by a fuel when it is burnt.

- **Coefficient**. A **constant** for a substance, used to calculate quantities related to the substance by multiplying it by other quantities. For example, the force pushing two materials together multiplied by the **coefficient of friction*** for the surfaces gives the **frictional force***.

- **Constant**. A numerical quantity that does not vary. For example, in the equation $E = mc^2$ (see also page 84), the quantity c (the speed of light in a vacuum) is a constant. E and m are **variables** because they can change.

- **Cosine** (of an angle). The ratio of the length of the side adjacent to the angle to the length of the hypotenuse (the longest side) in a right-angled triangle. It depends on the angle.

- **Inversely proportional**. When applied to two quantities, means that, for example, if one is doubled, the other is halved.

- **Mean**. A synonym for average, i.e. the sum of a series of values divided by the number of values in the series.

- **Medium** (pl. **media**). Any substance through which a physical effect is transmitted, e.g. glass is a medium when light travels through it.

- **Meniscus**. The concave or convex surface of a liquid, e.g. in water or mercury. It is caused by the relative attraction of the molecules to each other and to those of the container (see also **adhesion** and **cohesion**, page 23 and **parallax error**, page 102).

- **Proportional**. When applied to two quantities, means that they have a relationship such that, for example, if one is doubled, so is the other.

- **Rate**. The amount by which one quantity changes with respect to another, e.g. **acceleration*** is the rate of change of distance with time. Note that the second quantity is not necessarily time. If a graph of Y against X is plotted, the rate of change of Y with respect to X at a point is the gradient at that point.

- **Reciprocal**. The value obtained from a number when one is divided by it, i.e. the reciprocal of any number x is 1/x. For example, the reciprocal of 10 is 0.1.

- **Sine** (of an angle). The ratio of the length of the side opposite the angle to the length of the hypotenuse (the longest side) in a right-angled triangle. It depends on the angle.

- **Spectrum** (pl. **spectra**). A particular distribution of wavelengths and frequencies, e.g. the **visible light spectrum*** ranges from 4 x 10^{-7} to 7.5 x 10^{-7} m.

- **System**. A set of connected parts which have an effect on each other and form a whole unit.

- **Tangent** (of an angle). The ratio of the length of the side opposite the angle to the length of the side adjacent to it in a right angled-triangle. It depends on the angle.

- **Variable**. A numerical quantity which can take any value. For example, in the equation $E = mc^2$ (see also page 84), E and m are variables since they can take any value (although the value of E depends on the value of m). The quantity c (the speed of light in a vacuum) is a **constant**.

- **Volume**. A measurement of the space occupied by a body. See page 101 for calculations of volume. The **SI unit*** of volume is the cubic metre (m^3).

Index

The page numbers listed in the index are of three different types. Those printed in bold type (e.g. **79**) indicate in each case where the main definition(s) of a word (or words) can be found. Those in lighter type (e.g. 82) refer to supplementary entries. Page numbers printed in italics (e.g. *34*) indicate pages where a word (or words) can be found as a small print label to a picture.

If a page number is followed by a word in brackets, it means that the indexed word can be found inside the text of the definition indicated. If it is followed by (I), the indexed word can be found in the introductory text on the page given.

Bracketed singulars and plurals are given where relevant after indexed words. Synonyms are indicated by the word "See", or by an oblique stroke (/), if the synonyms fall together alphabetically.

119

Out of phase (waves), 38 (Phase)
Output (computers), 111
Overtones, 43 (Modes of
vibration)
Oxygen (O), 112

P

Palladium (Pd), 112, 114
Paper capacitor, 59
Parallax, 47
Parallax error, 102
Parallel (components), 64
Parallelogram rule, 108
Paramagnetism, 72
Parking orbit, see Geo-
stationary orbit
Partial eclipse, 47
Particle accelerators,
86 (Radioisotope)
Pascal (Pa), 24, 97
P.E., see Potential energy
Peaks (waves), see Crests
Penumbra, 46 (Shadow)
Perfect machine, 20
Period (T), 16, 34, 97
Natural, 17
Periodic motion, 16-17
Permanent magnets, 70 (Hard)
Permeability, 73
Phase (waves), 38
Phase difference, 38 (Phase)
Phons, 42 (Loudness)
Phosphorescence, 45
Phosphors,
45 (Phosphorescence)
Phosphorus (P), 112
Photomultiplier, 90 (Scintillation
counter)
Photons, 85 (Quantum theory)
Photosynthesis, 44 (Ultra-
violet radiation)
Physical quantities, 96 (I), 98, 99
Physical states, 4-5, 30-31
Pitch,
(mechanical), 21 (Screw jack)
(sound), 42
Planck's constant, 85
Plane coil, see Flat coil
Plane mirror, 47
Plano-concave, 53
Plano-convex, 53
Plastic, 22 (Electricity)
Plastic deformation, 23 (Yield
point)
Platinum (Pt), 112, 114

Plotting compass, 72 (Magnetic
field lines)
Plutonium (Pu), 112
Pnp transistor, 65, 110
Point(s),
Antinodal, see Antinodes
Boiling, 30 (Vaporization), 31
Fixed, 26
Focal, see Principal focus
Freezing, 30 (Freezing)
Ice, 26 (Fixed point)
Lower fixed, 26 (Fixed point)
Melting, 30 (Melting), 31
Neutral, 72
Nodal, see Nodes
Steam, 26 (Fixed point)
Upper fixed, 26 (Fixed point)
Yield, 23
Point action, 57
Point of incidence, 46, 50
Polarization, 68
Pole(s),
Consequent, 71
(magnets), 70
(mirrors), 48
North / North seeking, 70 (Pole)
South / South seeking,
70 (Pole)
Polonium (Po), 112
Polyester capacitor, 59 (Paper
capacitor)
Positrons, 86 (Beta particles),
87 (Beta decay)
Potassium (K), 112
Potential, 58, 106-107
Potential difference (V), 58,
97, 106-107
Potential divider, 63
Potential energy (P.E.), 8, 106-107
Elastic, 8
Electromagnetic, 8
Gravitational, 8
Molecular, 8
Nuclear, 9
Potential gradient, 58 (Potential)
Potentiometer, 63 (Variable
resistor), 110
Power (P), 9, 97
(lens), 53
Magnifying, see
Angular magnification
Power station(s), 61
Nuclear, 94 (I)
Praseodymium (Pr), 112
Preferential discharge, 66 (Ionic
theory of electrolysis)
Prefixes (units), 96
Pressure (P), 24-25, 97
Atmospheric, 24,
25 (Barometer)
Pressure law, 33
Pressurized water reactor
(PWR), 95

Primary cell, 69
Primary circuit, 78
Primary coil, 79
Primary colours, 55
Principal axis, 48, 52
Principal focus (F), 48, 52
Principle of flotation, 25
Principle of moments,
15 (Rotational equilibrium)
Principle of reversibility of
light, 49, 50
Principle of superposition, 39
Prism, 51
Probability clouds, see Orbitals
Progressive waves, 34 (I)
Projection lens (slide
projector), 54
Promethium (Pm), 112
Proof plane, 57
Properties (substances), 114
Molecular, 22-23
Thermometric,
26 (Thermometer)
Proportional, 115
Proportionality,
Limit of, 22 (Hooke's law)
Proportional limit, see
Limit of proportionality
Protactinium (Pa), 112
Protons, 82
P-shell, 83 (Electron shells)
P-type (semiconductor),
65 (Doping)
Pulley system, 20, 21
Pulse (Wulf) electroscope, 89
PWR, see
Pressurized water reactor

Q

Q-shell, 83 (Electron shells)
Quanta (sing. quantum),
85 (Quantum theory)
Quantities, 96-97, 113
Basic, 96
Derived, 97
Physical, 96 (I)
Scalar, 108
Vector, 108
Quantum theory, 85

We are grateful to the following
organizations for permission to
use their illustrations.

British Standards Institution (p.88)
NASA (p.93)
National Remote Sensing Centre
(p.45)
Royal Marsden Hospital (p.40)
Toshiba (pgs. 1 and 45)
UK Atomic Energy Authority (pgs.
1, 94 and 95)